NORTH

ENTRANCE FORECOURT

SERVICE COURTYARD

CHAPEL FORECOURT

PARTERRE
Gravel

OUTDOOR DINING
SPACE

DESIGNING GARDENS

DESIGNING

Arabella Lennox-Boyd

GARDENS

with Caroline Clifton-Mogg
Photography by Andrew Lawson

FRANCES LINCOLN

Frances Lincoln Limited
4 Torriano Mews
Torriano Avenue
London NW5 2RZ
www.franceslincoln.com

British Library Cataloguing-in-Publication Data
A catalogue record for this book is available from the British Library
ISBN 0 7112 1757 2

2 4 6 8 9 7 5 3 1

Designed by Jo Grey
Index by Marie Lorimer
Consultant on plant nomenclature Tony Lord

Printed and bound in Singapore

Contents

INTRODUCTION

During thirty years I have designed nearly three hundred gardens. Some of the projects have been very large and prestigious; others have been in extreme or unusual geographical conditions. But I do not believe that, to draw inspiration from this book, you need to have a garden large enough for a ha-ha or a maze, any more than you need to have the same conditions as an exotic foreign place. Visiting the grand gardens of historic houses can provide inspiration to the owners of gardens of any size, even a window box. So this book is for all who love plants and design, wherever they garden.

I have been fortunate enough to design many gardens around the world in a variety of landscapes – from Britain to the Americas, from the heat of the Tropics and the Mediterranean to the winter cold of Canada. I have written about that work, distilling the principles and ideas that have guided me and looking in detail at some of the gardens and the solutions I created to meet the very different challenges that each presented.

For me, the most important garden of all is my own in Lancashire. It has been a source of inspiration, and also something of an experimental station for other commissions. Gresgarth is not an easy garden, and for me it was by no means love at first sight. The house stands on the edge of the Artle Beck, a river that is frequently in spate: it runs from moorland, through several miles of semi-ancient woodland, into the garden. Steep hills, wooded mainly with oak, ash and beech, rise beyond the river and on three sides. After the hilltop home of my Italian childhood, with views stretching for miles in every direction, I found the idea of being at the bottom of an enclosed valley very oppressive. The rugged informality of the landscape posed an additional challenge: my natural inclination is towards symmetry, and it was clearly going to be difficult to impose symmetry here.

Moreover, it was evident from the beginning that the physical conditions of the site would complicate matters further: the garden lies in a frost pocket, the soil is heavy, the climate is wet and there is a powerful west wind that blows straight from the sea and eddies against the hills behind the house and through the wood. I had an early disappointment after we moved in, when I planted a collection of *Rhododendron augustinii*. These were devastated by three days of fierce wind, just as they were about to flower. This was a sharp lesson, one of many I have learned in the course of my twenty-two very practical gardening years at Gresgarth.

The new garden evolved as and when I needed to experiment. As my business grew it became apparent that I had to develop it carefully so that it could be used for publicity to promote my work. I also needed a place where I could try out different gardening techniques, planting ideas, plant combinations and designs, and Gresgarth became for me that place. Living and working there in all seasons, it is not possible ever to lose sight of the fact that a garden is a living, changing thing and not a static object. Gresgarth has therefore been invaluable in my work elsewhere.

Writing this book has been a pleasure: not only has it brought back to me the gardens I have so loved and still love being involved in, but it has confirmed in my mind my passion for design, my interest in nature and plants and, most importantly of all, my desire to create gardens that other people will themselves love and enjoy for the rest of their lives.

I have many people to thank for helping me with this book: all the clients who kindly allowed photographs of their gardens to appear in my book, Andrew Lawson for so sensitively capturing in his wonderful photographs the essence of my gardens, Sarah Mitchell for gathering all the loose ends and putting the disparate sentences in some sort of order, Jo Christian for editing the whole text so skilfully and Jo Grey for patiently choosing from hundreds of slides and producing a most glamorous book. I must also thank the wonderful team in my office, in particular Christopher Jordan who meticulously redrew nearly all the plans for the book; and, last but not least, my husband, Mark, for his constant support and for being so patient.

The house at Gresgarth, seen from the other side of the lake. Beds alongside the walls of the house and the terraces going down to the edge of the lake burgeon with rich planting, so that the house is seen as though rising from a mass of plants and flowers. *Rosa* 'Fritz Nobis' is in the foreground.

PRINC

GARDEN STRUCTURE

Top to bottom The overall simplicity of the planting here ensures that it does not compete with the house's handsome façade. In a grander setting, complex formal gardens and wide expanses of lawn are appropriate. Soft grasses and pleached limes gently mark a boundary between garden and grazing land.
Pages 8–9 Mown paths through long grass cross the parkland at Gresgarth between young planting that gives a foretaste of the mature design to come.

Although each garden is unique, there are some design principles that are generally applicable. My most passionately held principle is that a well-designed garden should relate to the wider landscape, and the transition from designed to natural should be subtle and imperceptible. It is important to acknowledge and use existing features or landmarks such as rivers, streams, contours, even railway lines. I always intend that when I have finished a garden, my intervention will look suitable and inevitable. I also strongly believe that you should feel compelled to visit every part of a garden: the design should lead you through.

Every garden should have a coherent narrative, for a garden that is disjointed is a garden that does not function. Even in the smallest garden you should want to move from one part to another, to be stimulated by different sensations and feelings, and to make discoveries that excite or calm. Each part of the garden should flow into the next in a harmonious way, with paths that encourage you to progress from area to area and views and focal points that visually entice you through. Among the elements that play a structural role in the garden, walls, hedges and pergolas create external and internal boundaries; trees, terraces, paving and pools make important features and focal points; and paths and steps articulate the whole skeletal framework. Added pleasure comes from surprises: perhaps a well-concealed secret garden, or a sculpture or structure that you come upon in an unexpected place.

Contemporary design must be original and adapted to modern ways and thinking, but it must also draw inspiration from the past. With this in mind, it is worth developing the habit of carefully observing – and making notes on – buildings, gardens and landscapes.

Assessing the site

Before starting the design for any new project I walk extensively round the site to get a feel of the place. Over the years I have found that my first impression, that instinctive and sometimes powerful message one gets from the initial visit, is the clue to follow. I obviously must also hear my clients' ideas and understand their needs and aspirations. What exactly do they want from their garden? How are they going to use it? How much help do they have in the garden? What is their budget?

I then assess the natural condition of the place and its surroundings, and make an appraisal of the physical aspects, such as the lie of the land, pleasing views, the overall climate, the prevailing winds. I also consider such negative factors as frost pockets, noise and less attractive views. When I have recorded these points (in some detail), I arrange for a full survey of the land, to show the existing levels, features and vegetation and any underground services there might be. This is vital, because when you merely survey a garden visually, distances and relationships can be missed or incorrectly assessed.

Next I look to see how the landscape beyond the garden can be used. Surrounding countryside and views can be borrowed to make the garden appear bigger. A ha-ha or an opening in a hedge will reveal the view; trees can be planted to frame a viewpoint and link into the landscape beyond. Another option is to design the garden as an integral part of the countryside immediately beyond its confines, by repeating inside the garden elements that appear outside: particular trees in the wider landscape, for example, might be mirrored within the garden, so that the eye sees a natural flow.

Archival research is also important at this stage, particularly if the house or the landscape is ancient or historic. In any case, regardless of the age of either house or garden, it is interesting and important to research the history of both. The more thorough the research, the more useful the exercise.

You can draw much inspiration and insight from such knowledge, even if a full historic restoration is not planned. I always make sure that all this information is noted on drawings of the site; more information is added as and when it is collected. This set of drawings makes up a sort of scrapbook of information, which is enormously helpful in the design process.

I am always mindful of the style of the house and the taste and character of my clients. In general, different styles of garden are appropriate for different architectural periods. For example, the clear, geometric lines of a classical or a modern building instinctively demand simplicity and a degree of space around the house; while architecture from other periods, for example the Victorian era or even the seventeenth century, often allows a more detailed or elaborate approach to the design of the areas next to the house. However, these are not hard and fast rules, for there are always many different possible solutions to every problem.

My design will of course be influenced by the size of the building. If the house is large, the design will be on a relatively large scale. The lie of the land, as well as the climate and location, will also affect the design. On a windy site, for instance, trees and hedges will play a major part in creating both enclosures and shelter; these sheltering plants can be arranged to create openings and views towards the countryside where appropriate.

By the time I start to think about the design in any detail I have a solid understanding of the place. The final proposal is shaped by a combination of my initial instinctive feeling and the information that is revealed by analysis of the site.

Filling in the design – hard and soft landscaping

When the master plan, with its gardens, landscaped walks, vistas and sitting areas, has been approved by the client, I begin to concentrate on the design of the hard landscape features, walls and paving details, steps and lighting, as well as other essentials such as drainage.

When I first think about the look of the garden I like to relate the design to trees and plants, and these can influence my design philosophy, but the

Top to bottom At Stanbridge Mill, the design of an intimate area next to the house, with its solid geometry of box contrasting with the soft, overflowing flowers of *Nepeta racemosa* 'Walker's Low', leads the eye through to the more open garden beyond. Also at Stanbridge, a rustic pavilion and timber walkway complement a naturalistic wetland planting that includes miscanthus and *Salix elaeagnos* subsp. *angustifolia*. Elaborate pillars supporting *Rosa* 'New Dawn' match the grandeur of this long wall at Eaton Hall.

Left to right I decided to make the planting at the edge of the garden at Las Navas informal and naturalistic, using plants like olive and cypress trees, so that it would merge imperceptibly into the surrounding wilder landscape. At the entrances of the rose garden at Thorpe Hall I placed two arches so they frame an enticing view of the garden beyond. In this enclosed space at Las Navas, a beautiful seat backed by a hedge of pittosporum and framed by a rose arch and a pretty planting of 'Iceberg' roses and *Ballota pseudodictamnus* focuses attention inward to the pool and the statue.

detailed planting plan comes at a much later stage. It evolves preferably after discussion with my clients; I like to make sure that I have correctly interpreted their tastes and desires.

The very last task is the choice, design and placing of the garden furniture, by which I mean pergolas and archways, and pots and tubs, as well as seats and tables. These are the finishing touches that give a garden extra character. As with all other aspects of the design, they must be of the highest quality, well detailed and perfectly adapted to each individual site.

Retaining the inspiration

Over the years, I have found that during the construction of the garden it is important – particularly on a long-term project – to remind myself from time to time of my initial judgment. Amidst the distractions of building regulations and other practical constraints, it is fatally easy to lose sight of that first intention.

I well remember how, during the lengthy construction of one particular project, which took three years to complete, I suddenly realized that I had completely lost the initial gut feeling of how I wanted the garden to look. So I went right back through all my papers, and looked again at the first photographs and asked myself why I had reached my chosen design solutions.

I realized then that, had I not thought to stop and reassess at that point, much of the simplicity and charm of the original vision would have disappeared.

Reason in design

Everything in a garden, every element involved, should be there not simply for its own sake, but because it is necessary. An avenue of pleached limes, for example, should be there as a definition of an area, as a windbreak or as a link between one building and another. A naturalistic planting or a wildflower meadow should be a response to the requirements of the design and the surrounding landscape. Indeed, the overall design of the garden itself and the siting of its different areas must be practical, dictated not only by the site and the house, but also by the particular wants and needs of the client and the growing requirements of the chosen plants.

A herb garden, for example, needs to be near the kitchen for quick access, and should be sited to receive the maximum amount of sun and heat for the plants; ideally it should be paved with stone or brick, which looks good with the plants and is practical to walk on, but one can also use gravel or hoggin, which, though not as crisp, provides good drainage. The vegetable garden need not be so near the kitchen. However, I like an early-flowering spring garden to be close to the house so that it can be seen in wet and cold spring weather without venturing too far outside. A woodland garden, on the other hand, can be farther away, because traditionally the woodland is part of the wider landscape beyond the immediate confines of the house. A herbaceous border can be sited either in the middle distance, making the focus of a pleasant summer walk, or nearer as a main vista to be viewed from the house. Swimming pools and tennis courts are usually best built at some distance or hidden away. A swimming pool can be made to look attractive – as at Ditchley where Geoffrey Jellicoe ingeniously designed one to look like a pond – but then all clutter must be discouraged. Everything that usually goes with a swimming pool – the furniture, toys and noise – is incompatible with the tranquillity of a garden.

steps and terraces

It makes sense to consider steps and terraces together. Both serve the function of linking and separating different areas – both physically and visually. One leads to another, they balance each other, and each provides a vital element of symmetry in the garden.

Steps

Garden steps are, in the most basic sense, practical necessities that enable one to move between different levels. But steps can also be interesting in their own right, challenging in design terms and a device that can make the garden livelier and more stimulating.

I have been very much influenced by the steps which Gae Aulenti designed for a villa in Florence; they have inspired me in many of my gardens. The design is very spacious, and the steps are of grass edged with light-coloured stone. This design fits the restrained simplicity of Florentine Renaissance architecture and has terrific strength and design impact. What I find exciting is that although the steps are formal, they follow the lie of the land in an irregular but geometric design, which is very contemporary.

On a large scale, Francesco de Sanctis, architect of the steps down to the Piazza di Spagna in Rome, used the differences of level to create monumental flights of steps which are linked by a succession of terraces. In a smaller way, at the Villa Garzoni at Collodi, near Lucca, and at Upton in Warwickshire, the same device of flights of steps and terraces has been used to link the upper gardens to the lower.

Above In this garden in Madrid I planted cypress trees to line the outer edges of the steps, both for decorative effect and to integrate them into the garden. Where the design is deliberately crisp with clean lines there is no need for too much planting to soften the hard surfaces, but neat shapes in adjoining beds and handsome stone or terracotta pots planted formally with topiary shapes will add the right ornamental touch. Here, the dark green of the clipped box balls and the soaring cypresses make a perfect contrast of shape and colour with the smooth, pale horizontals of the steps.

Opposite
Top left In a small garden you can make changes in level more interesting by demarcating them rather than just letting the land slope. These wide, terrace-like grass steps are edged with stone, and the horizontals make a pleasing contrast with the rounded forms of the planting.
Top right In a wilder or woodland setting, steps need to be informal. Here, timber poles provide a fittingly rustic edge to grass steps.
Centre left Sometimes it can be effective to break up a flight of steps with a wider landing or terraced area, to vary the rhythm. Here, the lower steps are also curved, pushing outward into the garden, and the stone is softened by planting spilling over the edges and colonizing the joints.
Centre right In this informal, jungle-like setting in Barbados, although the steps have been given definition by solid stone risers, the grass treads and the encroaching planting of Japanese iris help them merge into the lush greenery.
Below left If it is dramatic enough, a flight of steps can be a principal feature in a garden. I designed these for the garden at Las Navas, as a contemporary interpretation of the water cascade at the Villa Lante in Italy. The steps are made from cobblestones set in concrete, and clipped box shapes, representing the fish-like forms at the Villa Lante, line the fall of water.
Below centre A basket-weave pattern of bricks decorates a small terrace at the meeting of four routes through the garden. Terraces between flights of steps are useful for signalling a change of pace or direction.
Below right An exuberant mass of *Lonicera periclymenum* 'Munster' spills over the side wall of a flight of steps at Gresgarth, providing a romantic, fragrant counterpoint to the straight lines of stone.

In a garden where sharply rising ground means that the difference of level is great, long, shallow steps or ramps can be very powerful architectural elements. At the palace of the Vatican in Rome, visitors wishing to see the Pope had first to walk the length of the Sala Regia, which consisted of a shallow ramp that rose just enough to render the walker short of breath. This ramp was a theatrical device, designed for dramatic effect. The ramp was the design.

The design of steps can also be used to reflect the different uses and areas of the garden, or to convey a sense of formality or informality. Formal steps are usually made from stone or brick; if the steps are informal, the rises could be made from wood or irregular stones or pebbles or even old railway sleepers with the treads filled with gravel or coarse bark. A softer look can be achieved with grass steps that have been edged with stone or metal.

Steps should generally be at least as wide as the path to which they are linked and, unless there are space restrictions, the height of the rise should ideally be 9–10 centimetres (3½–4 inches), with a maximum height of 15 centimetres (6 inches) for steps close to the house. Further away from the house, the rise can be up to 20 centimetres (8 inches). I have occasionally been forced to have steps with a 20 centimetre rise near the house, but this is very steep. The higher the rise, the wider the step should be – a tread with a depth of 38 centimetres (15 inches) is generally comfortable.

Terraces

Gardens should not be designed just to be looked at. They are for living in, and you should be able to sit, to eat, drink, read and think in them. Terraces provide an ideal setting for all of these activities. A terrace near the house makes a transition between house and garden: in a hot country it adds enormously to the pleasure of both; in a country with changeable weather, like Britain, it is a practical necessity.

The influential garden designer Russell Page felt that levelled horizontal areas close to the house were an important component of all garden design, not least because they firmly place a house and suggest stability and rest. Ideally, a terrace near the house should be large enough at least to accommodate a table and chairs, as well as groups of pots with seasonal flowers or topiary shapes. Where the garden is large, there should also be plenty of space for borders. A generous terrace that is proportionate to the width and height of the house will visually anchor the building. Le Nôtre is said to have required that the depth of the space next to the house should be equal

to the height of the house, but most designers today would consider that excessive. For myself, the size of the terrace is more instinctive, depending on the space available around the house, though usually I am generous. The proportions of the terrace should also broadly relate to those of the area of land surrounding the house.

A terrace needs to be in a sunny position. Most, for pragmatic reasons, have a hard surface, though grass is an option if the architecture of the house suggests it. For example, an eighteenth-century house might need to sit in its landscape with little interruption. Equally, in a garden in a hot country a lawn terrace can be very agreeable. A grassy area near the house is a very attractive feature, provided that it is watered enough to keep it green.

A garden that is on a sloping site can have a series of terraces – indeed, all sloping gardens should be terraced if the space and levels allow. Each terrace can have a different character and use. In Mediterranean countries gardens often have such terraces, traditionally with retaining drystone walls, where crops such as olives and vines are grown. In a friend's house in Patmos where I spend blissful holidays, the garden is built on a series of stepped terraces, some entirely planted and others with wide paved areas. The main terrace is the largest and flanks the whole house. As you descend there are further terraces, some for sitting, one covered by a pergola for reading in the shade of the climbing vine, another for enjoying the evening light and the scent of jasmine, one with orange and lemon trees, and another with olive trees and a tangle of bougainvillea. Each terrace has a different character, with specially designed furniture to suit the use. This wonderful creation was initially the work of Teddy Millington-Drake and the garden is now further developed and improved by John Stefanidis. I have been greatly influenced by these friends' approach to design and always like to design a variety of different areas in my gardens, to encourage my clients to use the garden in their daily life.

I designed these very wide, very shallow steps for the outer garden at Château de Reux in Normandy. Their outline was inspired by steps created by the designer Gae Aulenti, which I had seen in Florence. The grass steps are staggered and edged with white stone, giving them the appearance of geometric waves as they flow down the contours of the land. They lead from an enclosed square lawn to a long rectangular pool surrounded by pleached hornbeam and are as simple, formal and contemporary as the design of the two garden rooms they link.

Paving is an important structural element in garden design. It can be used to contain and define and to lead the eye, to balance, contrast and complement areas of planting, as well as for purely decorative effect. It should always be carefully and imaginatively thought out – especially as most of us look down when we walk, and take pleasure from seeing a pattern beneath our feet. Paving always forms an integral part of my garden plans, and I pay great attention to the design.

Generally, surfaces made up of individual elements like stone, brick or granite setts are most effective, although concrete, with the flexibility it gives the design, can be beautiful if it is used properly and mixed with the appropriate aggregate. Concrete can also be effectively teamed with traditional paving materials such as stone, cobbles, flints, bricks and tiles. Extremely interesting paving patterns can be designed by using a combination of different materials. I have been much influenced by the attention to detail, and the imaginative use of materials, in Japanese paving patterns.

Usually the best paving designs are influenced by the place, character and history of the house. I try to use local materials when I can, for those that are natural to the area work better with the landscape and architecture. For example, at Stanbridge Mill, in Dorset, I designed patterns using local flint combined with brick. In Barbados, to reinforce the seaside theme, I used reproduction ammonites of different sizes as central patterns in the paths made from local coral stone.

Even a simple pathway presents an opportunity for a decorative effect, especially at a crossing. The larger the area of paving, the more important it is to break it up with some pattern. For example, a dining area can be visually contained by the design of the floor. If large containers are incorporated into the terrace, the paving design could include specially delineated areas for the pots.

The method of laying paving is important. Many builders seem not to differentiate between outdoor and indoor floors; indeed, it can be difficult to find a builder who understands that outdoor paving should be almost organic in appearance.

A lot of builders tend to go for the easy option of using concrete as a sub-base to paving, but I much prefer to use hard core with a weak mortar layer which includes lime for flexibility. This allows beds and borders to drain naturally. If, under duress, some concrete has to be used to hold the paving in place, then I specify that there should be no haunching on the side of the border. This way I can plant right up to the edge of the path. I do not like to see large cement joints on terraces or paths. I much prefer to have closely butt-jointed pavers with a dry mix of sand, cement and lime brushed into the hairline joints and then watered in to secure the paving.

Left, clockwise from top A bold 'S' in stone, contrasting with a background of granite setts laid in a swirling, circular pattern. A geometric design of brick, knapped (split) flint and tiles set on edge. A star of tiles laid on edge on a background of knapped flint, contained within a circle of brick. In this complex criss-cross design, round stones and pale-coloured Dutch bricks are attractively colonized by mosses. A collection of man-made ammonites which we set into squares and rectangles of coral-stone paving in Barbados. A geometric grid of squares and circles formed by stone slabs and edgings of black pebbles. A terrace of brick laid in a neat basket-weave pattern decorated with broad lines of knapped flint.
Below A formal, Japanese-inspired patio in Madrid with a highly decorative pattern of paving in a contemporary style. A terrace of geometrically cut local stone contains a central slate fountain surrounded by a square border of slate. Four symmetrically placed beds, planted with orange trees rising out of mounds of box, are edged with a broad square border of pebbles.

Paths are the garden's arteries – and one of the hardest things to get right. Although they can be used as design features or as part of a pattern, and as such can be objects of beauty, essentially they must be practical, and, on the whole, they should be unobtrusive. Their main purpose is to lead from one place to another. In formal situations, whether historic or contemporary, paths are usually straight. They can also form part of a pattern and in a simple garden the paths can be the basic structure of the garden. In an informal situation a path should never arrest the eye unless it leads to a focal point. If not carefully placed and sensitively designed, a path can add an unwelcome man-made or urban feel to a natural or rural setting.

Paths must be sited with care. Except in formal designs, they should always follow the contours of the landscape, in a serpentine curve unmarred by sharp edges or straight lines. An informal path can be channelled within the contours of the garden so that it is for the most part unseen; it is best where possible to raise the level of the grass on the side where the path would be most easily visible, or to route it at a slightly lower level than the surrounding land. It can also be hidden by informal planting or hedging.

The choice of materials used to make a path depends on the style of the house and garden, the local materials and the purpose for which the path has been designed. In my opinion grass paths should be preferred wherever practical, as they are so attractive: the contrast of height and texture of the grass gives a garden a very natural feeling. Where conditions are reasonably dry, a grass path can be made simply by close-cutting a passage through long grass, the longer grass at either side of the path being cut at varying heights to give interest and relieve monotony. In wetter areas grass paths need to be laid on a base of sand and given proper drainage. Another practical solution for a grass path in a wet area, or for a path that is subject to heavy wear, is to lay stepping stones along the path, forming an attractive pattern. If you want to have a grass path in mottled shade, you will need to sow a woodland grass seed mixture; grass will not work at all in deep shade.

Similarly, while in drier areas woodland paths can be left to develop naturally, allowing leaf covering and natural woodland debris to form the paths, in wetter areas it is important to make sure that the drainage is efficient, and essential to have a solid base on which either woodland litter or bark can be layered. In woodland settings where there are steep slopes, hoggin paths work well; they are soon colonized by mosses and low grasses, which makes them look completely natural.

I find hoggin a very useful material for paths. At Eaton Hall, for example, all the paths I designed are made of a very thin

layer of gravel over a base of hoggin. This combination – used in many gardens in France but only occasionally in England – makes a path that is attractive and easy to maintain.

Brick paths are softer than stone and look less formal because they mellow and the surface eventually becomes colonized with moss. You can also have fun designing interesting patterns with bricks, either by varying the way you lay them or by mixing them with stone, cobbles, flints or tiles on edge. However, although brick makes a softer path, I would not normally use it in an area where stone is the local material.

Stone paths, which are, of course, definitely formal, can look magnificent if beautifully designed and detailed. However, a newly cut stone path will always look modern and crisp, so you should only use new stone when that is what you want to achieve. For a more mellow effect, recycled stone can be used. I avoid crazy paving if I can, except sometimes in Mediterranean countries: it can look very pretty there, in an informal situation, but I find that English gardens need the elegance and simplicity of a clean-cut terrace or path to set them off.

There is also an Italian and – particularly – Spanish tradition of mixing stone with white and black pebbles and making elaborate patterns. In a garden I designed in Marbella we called upon a father and son whose family had for generations made pebbled patterns for all the most famous gardens in Spain. It was a privilege to observe and learn from these wonderful craftsmen.

Granite setts are not often used for paths, but they can be interesting if mixed with stone in a formal layout, or used to edge a path. As well as forming an attractive pattern, they will provide a useful drainage channel. They can also be used in larger areas where there is vehicle traffic. They can often be seen laid in interesting patterns in European cities, especially in Rome.

Far left In an Italian garden, inset rectangles of pebbles packed together vary the pace of this herb garden path made of squares of bricks laid on end. The right-angled shapes in the paving contrast with the rounded forms of clipped chamaecyparis and the mauve flower heads of chives.
Centre At Gresgarth, large stone slabs provide a path through the garden. The planting softens the formality of the design, and the predominantly mauve-pink flower colour is sympathetically set off against the pale grey of the stone. Clipped box as edging and topiary shapes make a dark backing for the paler foliage of chamaecyparis, the soft shades of *Geranium ibericum* and *Allium cristophii* and the dark pink leaves of *Prunus cerasifera* 'Nigra'.
Below I am particularly fond of mown grass paths through meadows and plantings of longer grasses, like the *Stipa gigantea* shown here. They look very natural, and the contrast between the neat green ribbon of path and the cloudy fronds of tall grasses and flowers is very pleasing.

A well-built and attractive wall is a bonus without equal in a garden: it adds another dimension to the design, creates a microclimate, and acts as an excellent foil for both climbers and planting in the beds at its foot.

Walls provide architectural divisions in settings where a hedge would be inappropriate and are particularly well suited to town gardens and those where a high degree of shelter from the wind is needed. Walls do, however, create an eddy, so if the wall is in the lee of the wind, ensure that you plant trees or shrubs to deflect the wind before it hits the wall. Walls are particularly useful in small gardens where they take up less space than a hedge and can serve as another planting surface, for climbers and wall shrubs.

The height of a wall affects the sense of enclosure in a garden: high walls cut off the surrounding area and give a sensation of containment and secrecy; a low wall, on the other hand, while still imparting a feeling of enclosure, allows the presence of a world beyond, and can direct the eye towards a particular view.

Walls can be built from conventional stone or brick or in imaginative constructions in which these elements are combined in patterns with other materials like flint, pebbles, roof slates or even concrete. They are usually best built in materials that are traditional to the area, but in some situations it can be attractive to plaster and colour them to tie in with the architecture of the house or to make a focal point. In general, any wall that is attached to the house should be of the same material, but further out towards the landscape I like to use drystone walls or walls that are faced with stone.

Stone walls can be sculpturally beautiful; they can even be an artistic form, as the sculptor Andy Goldsworthy has demonstrated with his stone wall designs and drystone enclosures in Cumbria. There is a discernible difference between a drystone wall, which is organic and almost fluid, and which allows for drainage in a natural manner, and a stone wall made with cemented joints, which is more stiff and unyielding.

Brick walls are quite grand and can be very beautiful. I feel that they should always be built in the traditional way, and there is an amazing range of traditional patterns and combinations available.

Fences can also be useful and attractive. In the garden at Ascott House, which was very long and narrow, I divided the area into sections using low open fences with very pretty finials and espaliered trees or honeysuckle growing up against them. Handsome fences can also be made of wattle, which is a very effective screen, particularly around a vegetable garden where you need shelter, or around areas you may want to hide. Provided it is at least 1.5 metres (5 feet) high, a wattle fence also makes a good defence against sheep, cattle or deer. So it can be used as a practical as well as a design solution.

An iron fence can make a good boundary: it is unobtrusive and does not stop the eye, but allows the vision to flow out over the wider landscape.

Top left At Ascott House I used open wooden fencing to separate the many enclosures that I made in the long, narrow gardens round the house. To make the fence more interesting, I designed decorative round finials for the vertical posts, and had the whole fence painted black to match the black timbers of the house. Up against the fence I placed plants, such as espaliered apples, suited to the particular garden room. Against these two fences, which line the path between the black-and-white garden and the brown garden, are clumps of *Heuchera micrantha* var. *diversifolia* 'Palace Purple' and *Weigela florida* 'Foliis Purpureis', and the vista is edged with mounds of *Hebe subalpina*.

Top right The path leads out to the fields beyond at a lower level than the garden, thus providing well-drained conditions for pale green, silver-leaved and white-flowered plants such as *Lavandula angustifolia* 'Alba', artemisias, helianthemums, *Rosa* 'Iceberg' and the very double and quartered R. 'White Meidiland', and, at the back, *Euphorbia mellifera*.

Right We took down this old Cumbrian slate stone wall and reconstructed it in one of my Chelsea gardens. The aesthetic quality of a drystone slate wall is very different from that of other stone walls; it is more layered, and it can have straighter, more geometric edgings. Here, clipped topiary yew shapes stand sentinel either side of a neat opening, where an urn positioned as an eye-catcher nestles in a clump of *Viburnum opulus*, tempting you into the woodland beyond the doorway.

GARDEN STRUCTURE walls and fences

openings: gates, doors and arches

A gate in a garden is a focal point that entices you in or shuts you out. It can be used to enclose an area or to draw the eye forward and direct the attention to a point beyond. A solid door is a stronger statement – an opening into a very enclosed space, or into a walled garden, or a place where you want to hide something.

You should be aware that if you live in a frost pocket you definitely need a gate rather than a door: an open design will let the frost escape.

Windows or openings in gates or doors will focus the eye and add an air of mystery or secrecy, marking a boundary and yet allowing views or glimpses further into the garden. In some situations it is interesting simply to have a stone or brick arch as an opening to indicate a change of place or a sense of moving from one area to another. This can also direct the eye through the arch-frame and beyond to a point in the further landscape. The Chinese and Japanese used this device successfully with their Moon Gates.

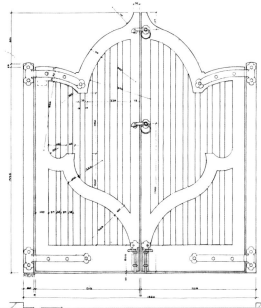

A gate should be appropriate to its setting and its design can be simple – even rustic – or elaborate and formal, as occasion demands; the design can range from a single set of wooden bars to a pair of elaborate, painted and gilded wrought-iron gates. Although I usually prefer wooden gates, as they seem to me less formal, in some instances metal gates can be particularly successful. For example, in both Spain and Barbados I use metal for many garden features, because the local metalwork is so good.

I like wooden gates to be painted, because this allows a little frivolity. Particularly in northern climates, a splash of colour can be very welcome as a relief from the monotony of the winter months.

Above, from left to right I designed this handsome pair of wooden gates for the kitchen garden at Gresgarth, giving it a solid base and close vertical bars so as to hide the working area beyond. A highly decorative gate I designed for the garden at Las Navas, displaying the fine metalwork of Spanish craftsmen. A design for a simple wooden gate for a smaller opening. The Leaf Gate, a more open and elaborate gate at Gresgarth, and my design for it. A wooden gate of trelliswork and cross-pieces set into a yew hedge at Belvedere.
Below, from left to right A diamond-pattern driveway gate at Gresgarth with imposing pointed Gothic gateposts inspired by a friend's garden. A simple openwork wooden gate leading into the surrounding fields at Stanbridge Mill. Two views of a Gothic gate inset in an archway in the kitchen garden wall at Gresgarth.

bridges and the ha-ha

Bridges

I enjoy designing bridges because they can be so varied in both form and use. They not only serve a practical purpose, they can also make a design feature or a focal point. They can be built in wood, metal or stone, and range from a simple slab of stone to take you across a small stream to a large, elaborate structure that has great impact on the landscape.

A bridge can reflect the character of the garden. At Gresgarth, for example, where the landscape is very powerful and rugged, I have built a sturdy bridge to withstand the bad floods we get regularly after a stormy spell. The bridge supports are massive but well hidden; the uprights are larger

than usual, but the panels in between are made of smaller sections so as to give a more delicate feel. I painted the upright posts and finials red, to bring a note of cheer on a glum northern winter's day.

In the milder climate of Dorset, at Stanbridge

Clockwise from top A simple rustic bridge connects watermeadows at Stanbridge Mill. The bridge in two colours at Gresgarth displays my love of painted woodwork in the garden, the red posts contrasting with the pale pink colour of the *Malus floribunda* behind. A picturesque stone bridge crosses a stream surrounded by an informal planting of ferns and *Zantedeschia aethiopica*. Two more bridges span the waterways at Stanbridge, but they are much more elaborate – similar in style, though one is very large, the other a small footbridge – since they cross the water from the cultivated garden near the house.

Mill, I was able to indulge in designing a variety of different bridges: a large one over the river and smaller ones in other areas of the garden, with still more in the watermeadows. All the bridges near the house are designed with attractive panels and pretty finials, while the bridges throughout the watermeadows are of simple rustic design. In this softer landscape I use no colour, because I do not want to introduce any distraction that might take away from the beauty of the natural surroundings.

The ha-ha

The ha-ha – which is in essence an invisible ditch – was first seen, like so many other formal garden features, in France, at Versailles (where it was known as an ah-ah), and the device was soon employed by designers across Europe. The first ha-ha in England was built during the late seventeenth century in the formal garden of Levens Hall in the north-west of England and was supposedly designed by M. Beaumont, a pupil of Le Nôtre. Otherwise surrounded by high walls, the garden of Levens has a small ha-ha which opens up a view on to a lime avenue that leads into the rural landscape beyond.

The ha-ha allows both the countryside and the view beyond to become an intrinsic part of the garden, while still permitting farming and agricultural activity to take its natural course. It is a practical way of connecting to a larger panorama without the visual interruption that would be imposed by a fence or another vertical boundary; it gives a feeling of space while encompassing the agricultural landscape.

A ha-ha can be as wide as you like; the depth, however, should be decided on the basis of what it is that you want to keep out – cattle, for example, can only be kept out of a garden by building quite a deep ditch.

A ha-ha need not be expensive to construct. If its walls are not immediately visible, it can be built in breeze blocks painted black or brown. Or, as I have recently done, you can cut it directly into the natural chalk: the chalk acts as a wall and is soon covered in mosses, lichen and wildflowers.

The ha-ha is supposedly named for the exclamation of surprise elicited when the hitherto invisible boundary is revealed; if it is well designed, it can also look natural from the 'visible' side, as does this ha-ha at Stanbridge Mill, simply cut out in the chalk and discernible only as the dark line of an overgrown ditch. Keeping animals out without intrusive fences, it allows a magnificent vista from the garden, over fields to a distant tower.

pergolas and arbours

Of the garden structures that provide support for plants, pergolas and arbours are the most architectural, and, to me, the most delightful. A pergola is a covered walk or open tunnel over which climbing plants can be trained, an arbour a shelter, usually round or square, that is shaded by plants. Both can be made of various materials, metal and wood being the most popular choices.

A pergola is a substantial feature that can have great impact in the garden and care must be taken in its design and placing. It is important to understand the volume of the overall design and to decide whether the pergola is to be its central feature. A pergola can, for example, surround a large square of grass, as a cloister might surround an internal garden. I have designed in Italy a wooden pergola surrounding a rather wide grass area, which gently rises to a central point at which there is a well. A monastery nearby has a cloister which inspired me; I wanted to re-create that peaceful feeling, particularly as the house is in beautiful countryside, and is surrounded by magnificent views over the hills.

If a structure with design impact is required, a pergola can be very large, and should preferably be made from wood; it might even have square or cylindrical pillars of stone or brick – a style that was much used by Gertrude Jekyll in her garden designs of the early twentieth century. For a less obtrusive structure, choose metal and paint it black or grey.

Arbours tend to be incidental features, rather than the linch-pin of a design, but can have be highly effective nonetheless, when used to provide a sitting place, make a focal point, or mark the intersection of two paths.

Clockwise from central drawing My design for a side panel for an arbour with a circular 'window'. A wide, open metal pergola makes a perfect support for *Wisteria floribunda* 'Alba', allowing the racemes to be seen at best advantage. A design for a roofed wooden arbour. An ornate metalwork arbour on a scale to match its battlemented surroundings is evocative of a medieval tented pavilion. A classically inspired metalwork arbour painted dark green to blend into a shady green and white garden in Paris. A handsome wooden arbour I designed both to shade an equally handsome seat and as a focal point at the end of a vista. I designed this pretty wooden pavilion in the Barbados garden to match the local plantation architecture of the house. I had this wooden shingle-roofed pergola made in the local Bajan (Barbadian) style of other wooden structures in the garden and positioned it at a pivotal point so that its cross-shaped arms link the main house with a new drawing room and the two main paths in the garden. An ornate metalwork support we call the bandstand, at Gresgarth. A romantic wooden arbour.

GARDEN STRUCTURE
climbing structures

Clockwise from above left Trellis is used to enclose separate garden rooms while allowing glimpses through. At Eaton Hall, I designed a row of wood and trelliswork columns connected by rope swags and decorated by urns, to support the climbing rose 'New Dawn'. An enclosing wall of painted trellis with panels connecting trelliswork columns for the Ritz Hotel in London. A design for a trellis arch with decorative finials. One arm of the wooden pergola covered with *Thunbergia grandiflora* that encloses a trellis by the pool in a garden in Spain.

Opposite, top to bottom Massive ornamental trellis pyramids provide structure and support for climbing roses at Eaton Hall. Trellis panels enclose a seat at Château de Reux. A row of decorative rose arches provides vertical structure in a regular rhythm for a rose garden in Yorkshire.

Vertical plant supports serve a variety of functions in the garden. As well as hosting climbing plants, they are a useful means of providing height or a framework, especially in areas where there are no trees. They can offer privacy, make an eye-catching focal point, or bring a sense of order.

Climbing structures are made in a wide range of different materials and shapes: they may be metal pyramids – tall and thin or wide and squat – wooden posts (usually oak or, in Mediterranean countries, chestnut), driven in the ground in a pyramid shape or as a pillar. A simple tall wooden stake will support a short clematis or one of the smaller roses. Bamboo canes can be arranged like a ladder, the horizontals tied with thick black string. You can make an attractive basket-like pyramid by driving hazel branches, 2.5 metres (8 feet) tall, in the ground in a circle, tying the top tight together to hold the twigs in shape and weaving the side twigs in. A simple pyramid can be made of thin branches tied at the top with willow. Metal arches are usually preferable to wooden ones, except in very informal situations, where you might use a wooden arch. Metal can, of course, be bent more easily than wood, and metal arches are more graceful.

Trellis is a traditional material for climbing structures. It is particularly useful in an urban garden, where its openwork lattice structure can enclose and create separate areas, while allowing visual access to other parts of the garden. It can be used as a framework along a wall or as plant-clad fencing, making divisions and enclosure in the garden. It can also be used to build openwork garden contructions such as gazebos and pavilions, designed with an entrance and perhaps windows or openings that either look out to views and the countryside, or are focused on points of interest – perhaps a border, or a sculpture or urn. Trellis can be designed in varying lattice widths, suitable for different purposes. A trellis with a dense, narrow lattice design is appropriate where a sense of enclosure and privacy is needed, and an airier lattice when a more open aspect is preferable. Combining trellis of different lattice widths can give an appearance of light and shade. Trellis can also be painted. If it is to be used in a country garden or principally as a foil for climbers, then it is best left in its natural state. But if it is to be a design feature – perhaps in a city garden – then it should definitely be painted. A very dark green is an effective colour, particularly for covering high brick walls; in Paris it is the traditional colour for trellis. But you can also use your imagination and experiment with other colours. Painted trellis, perhaps coloured in soft blue-green or grey-green, looks particularly effective against a white wall. This is good for small town gardens, where one wants as much light as possible.

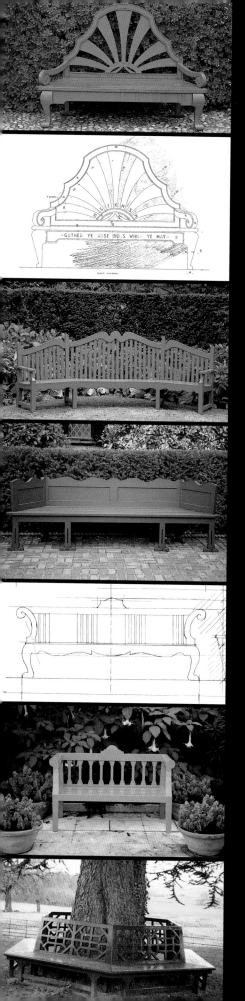

GARDEN
STRUCTURE furniture

When designing a garden, I always plan places to sit, as these are vital for fully appreciating the garden. Practically, such places provide somewhere to relax or entertain outside; ideally, one should be near the house – you will be taking cushions outside, and food and drink if you're entertaining, so you don't want to be far from the house – and flat and paved. But places to sit are also important structurally. Seating can make punctuation points that both lead you round the garden and then make you stop, perhaps to look at a view or back at the house. If a seat is an antique or particularly beautiful it can be used in an ornamental way, like a sculpture or an urn, as a feature or a focal point. You should always pay careful attention to the placing of furniture: insensitively positioned furniture which looks obtrusive can spoil a well-designed garden.

Within the garden, as opposed to by the house, a seat is best backed with something, such as a hedge or a grouping of shrubs. Sometimes – especially in a sunny climate – it is nice to be enclosed, to sit within an arbour or under a pergola.

Generally when designing a garden I like to choose the garden furniture, and ideally I like to design it. A bench can be as simple as a plank of wood or a stone slab, although for dining outside I feel that a formal design of tables and chairs looks best. Painted furniture suits some gardens particularly well. There are so many wonderful subtle colours to choose from. I would always go for a pale colour.

Left, top to bottom A seat following the pattern of a nineteenth-century seat once owned by the novelist Edith Wharton, for the garden at Las Navas. My design for the seat. A wing version of the style of seat known as the Olympia. A black-painted seat, solid but decorative, in the black-and-white garden at Ascott. Another design for a seat at Ascott. A seat inspired by one seen in Istanbul, with matching terracotta pots filled with *Kalanchoe pumila*. Inspired by an existing seat at Ascott, I designed this adaptation of an original Chinese fretwork seat to surround this ancient cedar.

Opposite, clockwise from top left Elegant deck chairs and a matching wooden table on a small terrace. A high-backed settle-style seat with cubes of box in front on either side. I copied this metal and wood seat from an antique French original. A gothic seat I designed for a London garden, with pyramids of small-leaved ivy either side and matching pots at its feet. An Olympia seat, backed by a yew hedge. A seat designed to be placed in each of the rose gardens at Eaton Hall – the one here has matching antique pots filled with white tulips on either side. A wooden seat at Stanbridge: it is painted with grey-coloured protective paint to blend in with the soft surrounding planting of *Iris* 'Blue Rhythm', lavender, saxifrage and, behind the yew hedge, clouds of *Crambe cordifolia*.

GARDEN STRUCTURE

ornament

Ornaments can help focus a garden, fixing your attention and even, by careful placement, conveying you round the garden. Drawing close to a beautiful statue, for instance, you might catch a glimpse of another one, which leads you on further. I like statuary to be unexpected – even oversized or incongruous – so that there is an element of excitement when you see it for the first time and you are surprised or amused. Natural, found objects such as wonderfully shaped boulders or a sculptural tree root can be ornamental in this way. Contemporary sculpture is effective in a garden. Modern materials such as polished steel and glass are very good at reflecting light and colours, adding a sensuous touch.

If an area of the garden needs emphasizing or reinforcing, I like to place ornamental objects, such as urns or outsized terracotta pots, regularly in a border or along a path, to create a sense of rhythm.

Left, clockwise from top A stone lion by the lake at Gresgarth, with tulips 'White Triumphator' and 'Spring Green' in the foreground. A beautiful Roman marble top placed on an ivy-covered plinth, surrounded by long grass and cow parsley in the birch wood at Stanbridge Mill. An eighteenth-century urn mounted on a modern column of slate and stone and, behind, the ruins of a stone tower brought to Gresgarth after I had used it in my Chelsea garden of 1993. A modern sculpture under towering *Pinus pinea*, part of a collection displayed against a wild backdrop at Las Navas in Spain.

Right, top to bottom A tufa stone obelisk down which water trickles at Gresgarth. A cobbled frog by Maggie Howarth in one of the small pools at Gresgarth. A limestone ball at No. 1 Poultry. 'Owl', a water organ designed by my husband, Mark, at Gresgarth: its owl-like hoot is produced by a water-powered spring. A stone horse sculpted by Belinda Eade out of a solid piece of stone, emerging from a cascade in a Mediterranean garden.

Page 36, clockwise from top left A stone Janus on an ivy-covered pillar (a good 'trick', as the pillar need not be of stone). A copy of the original Calydonian boar at Gresgarth – whose name means 'enclosure of the wild boar'. A stone bust set low in an informal base of box. A bowl sundial serving as a birdbath overlooks the river at Gresgarth. A formal urn on a base surrounded by box clipped to look like a formal pediment.

containers

Pots are essential in a garden. To me, a terrace, especially, looks undressed without planted pots or containers, and they are so important for adding seasonal interest. They can be planted with clipped evergreens for all-year-round effect, or they can be planted to change through the seasons – for example, with spring tulips that emerge through winter-flowering pansies, followed by annuals and tender perennials that extend the flowering season until autumn.

I much prefer to place pots and containers in a regular, balanced arrangement, for instance repeated on both sides of a path, or to position them in a formal framework – as a focal point at the end of a vista, for example. I particularly like to have pots planted with box shapes or with standard Portugal laurel on either side of an entrance.

I like containers to be colourful, not only in their planting but in themselves. Simple lead containers are handsome, and terracotta looks especially good in a warm climate such as the Mediterranean, but I especially enjoy using painted wooden containers and glazed pots in bright colours, to bring a touch of gaiety to the garden. In Barbados I was amused to design oversized pots made of coral stone.

Below left This ornate Tuscan terracotta pot makes an impressive centrepiece in the brown garden at Ascott House. The long spiky leaves of a purple *Cordyline australis*, framed by a metal arch clothed with *Rosa* 'Guinée' and *Vitis vinifera* 'Purpurea', make a striking contrast of form with the surrounding planting, including the rounded shapes of clipped purple beech, *Salvia officinalis* 'Purpurascens' and epimediums.

Below right Pots containing evergreen topiary shapes are particularly effective, and useful for year-round decoration. On the main terrace at Ascott – a garden once renowned for its topiary – I placed terracotta pots, filled with box clipped in wedding-cake-like tiers. They nestle in between more clipped box, this time grown in the borders and formed into spirals on solid square bases, and yew shaped into separate tiers. The topiary theme is continued in the background, with standard *Prunus cerasifera* 'Nigra' growing within blocks of boundary yew hedge.

Right, above The sprawling tendrils and pale-variegated leaves of *Helichrysum petiolare* 'Variegatum' look fresh and charming in a simple terracotta pot, and the foliage sets off the yellow flowers of *Argyranthemum* 'Jamaica Primrose' and the blues of *Agapanthus* Headbourne hybrids and *Campanula pyramidalis* behind. Although I usually prefer containers in regular, balanced arrangements, they can look very pretty clustered together in an informal grouping on a terrace.

Right, below A thin-lipped metal container is placed in a bed and filled with the same spring blooms that surround it, making it appear that *Tulipa* 'Prinses Irene', *Erysimum cheiri* 'Vulcan' and blue forget-me-nots have continued spilling out of the crowded pot into the bed below. Raising the planting in this way adds vertical interest and structure to a mass of flowers grown informally in a bed or border.

Far right, top to bottom *Fritillaria imperialis* 'Rubra Maxima' makes a dramatic display in a large basket. *Tulipa* 'Queen of Night' with touches of pale yellow wallflowers fill a simple stone container. The beautiful shape of this terracotta basket is enhanced with an upright planting of striped tulips 'Union Jack' that does not obscure the graceful lines of the bowl. A wide bowl looks better with planting that overflows, as it does in this example, set on an elaborate pedestal, which complements the formal setting of the Dragon Fountain Garden at Eaton Hall and is exuberantly planted with *Helichrysum petiolare* in flower.

Water has always been important in garden design and it has been very influential in my own design ideas. I was brought up in Rome, where water is everywhere, and used in every possible manner. There are formal fountains, basins and nymphaea round almost every corner; in the Italian countryside, in historical gardens such as Villa Lante, Villa d'Este and Villa Farnese at Caprarola water is the central, extravagant element, uniting the whole garden, and used for sound and reflection, as well as for cooling.

But although I was used to water as an element of formal garden design, it was not until I saw, in England, the lakes built in the eighteenth century as part of the landscape gardens that I realized how magnificent a large informal piece of water could be. Water brings so much life with it – the birds, the vegetation, the huge reflections and the vast depth. The romantic landscape has a very natural way of dealing with big expanses of water, contrasting with the formal stretches of water in French gardens such as Versailles and Courances. For smaller gardens both types of water – the formal and the informal – can be scaled down into a smaller landscape, as part of an overall design.

However, water is not easy to design or to maintain, particularly in an informal situation. An informal piece of water – a

a small garden it can make a very strong statement: in one garden I designed, for example, the space was almost entirely taken up by water, save for a single modern sculpture.

A water feature cannot be placed just anywhere, without thought; it must be part of a design. In a formal layout you must have a formal pool (though formal does not, of course, necessarily mean designed with straight lines), while as you move away from the formal areas of the garden the design can become more relaxed.

In a small garden, where, with few exceptions, a clear sense of structure is desirable, it is usually best if a formal pool has a geometric shape – perhaps a square, a rectangle or a hexagon. Water used in this way becomes a defined architectural space where the designer's ideas can be imposed.

Water can be used to lead the eye from one place to another. At Las Navas in Spain, for example, I designed a water feature where the water starts in one garden pool and gently flows down a staircase to another, providing sound and movement as it runs; flowing water is particularly desirable in hot countries, as it cools the air, and sounds refreshing.

And – why not – water can also be used to give amusement,

pond or a lake – must be in a depression in the land; it must look as if it has gathered there naturally, following a natural route. The same applies to a formal water feature: it must be placed where you get maximum reflection, at the end of a vista or a walk or a place you look into or over into; it must be a central feature of an area, and have plenty of flat land around it. A *pièce d'eau* must always sit comfortably in the landscape.

Water is a good feature to have in a town garden, giving as it does a sense of space by reflecting the sky and the surrounding plants; the sound of water can also help to mask traffic noise. In

as it was in Italy with the *giochi d'acqua* – hidden jets of water set off when an unsuspecting victim walked over them. There is a charming example of this in Rome, at the Quirinale, the former royal palace. A small, round, paved garden surrounded by hedges entices you in; as you walk on to the central paving, which is covered with exquisite mosaic patterns, you find yourself surrounded and enclosed by very fine water jets which rise unexpectedly from the floor.

However, when water is used in a more natural setting it is important to keep that simple feeling, to let nature speak. The

GARDEN **water** STRUCTURE

Far left A swimming pool needs to be carefully planned and discreetly sited if it is to look good in a garden. This pool was dug within an area bounded by an existing yew hedge; water flows down a canal and under the yew arch to a second pool, which is hidden from the house by a hedge.

Left Smooth lawns sweep down to the water's edge in this corner of the lake at Gresgarth, adding to the air of tranquillity. A willow and, on the left, tiered branches of *Cornus controversa* stand above the still water and add their green reflections.

Above Two lines of *Pterocarya fraxinifolia,* on either side of this quiet canal, lead the eye to the winged sculpture at the foot of the wooded hill.

Below left Water channels from the River Allen run through the grassy watermeadows at Stanbridge Mill. Here, a swathe of *Cortaderia richardii* planted on the meadow bank displays its pale feathery fronds.

Below right Lush tropical planting envelops the pool in this Barbados garden. In the foreground are the glossy leaves of a water hyacinth.

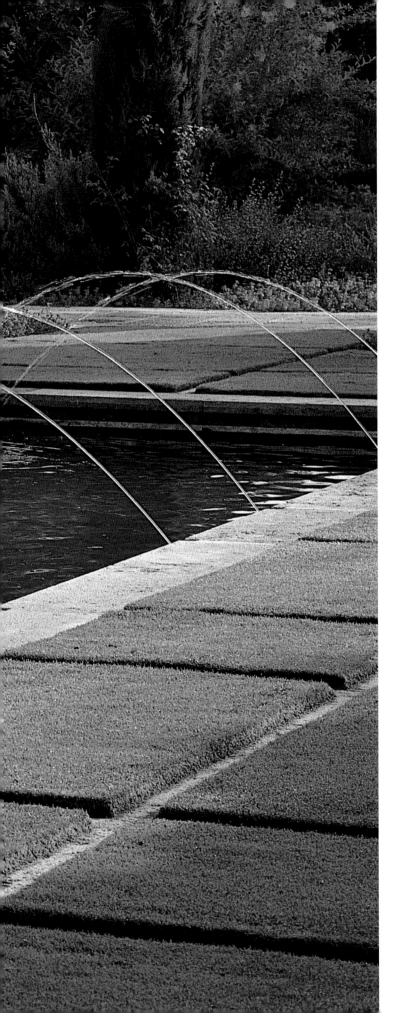

lake at Gresgarth, for example, is a water catchment, which was originally a medieval farm pond. When we first arrived the pool had no impact on the landscape and looked rather dull. I decided to enlarge it and yet keep it looking like a natural part of the landscape, to make it seem as though the nearby river had overflowed into the garden, forming a small lake. Today, it is a major feature that is visible from the house. Its reflective stillness is in stark contrast to the sound and movement of the river, which can sometimes be so violent as to overflow its banks.

In any design that includes flowing water, thought must be given to the speed of the flow. The faster the water flows, the more artificial it will look. Decide whether there will be waterfalls, whether it should flow at a gentle trickle or as a rushing stream (such considerations will determine the size of the pump).

The path of a stream, however small, must naturally always go down hill, following the contours of the land. It might be a quiet stream which meanders gently down the hill, or it might be like a stream in a Japanese garden where the water moves from one pool to another by way of waterfalls or cascades.

A more formal stream might be designed in the form of a rill – a narrow rectangular, shallow channel of the type often seen in Moorish and Mogul gardens and used to link one pool with another. A canal is larger than a rill – a formal, narrow rectangular pool, designed either on its own or as one of several, as at Courances in France. If you are designing a water feature away from the house, it must be far enough away and quite deep, as the eye foreshortens it. You must also be sure that it is far enough away from buildings to reflect the sky – otherwise the water will look dark and gloomy.

The style of the area around a piece of water should be dictated by whether the water is designed as a naturalistic or a more formal feature. Formal water should be surrounded by a crisp edge, which might be either of stone or of well-clipped grass edged with stone or metal. An artificial informal pool looks more natural if the edges are planted with moisture-loving plants of the sort that would naturally colonize the water margins. One must be aware that the edges of a man-made water feature will not necessarily be damp, and you may have to ensure that water permeates the soil to make a boggy area. Remember, too, that water gardens and damp borders need to be kept under control, since permanently damp soil encourages weeds to proliferate.

Jets of water add a Moorish feel to this contemporary formal pool bordered by a lawn inlaid with a geometric pattern of stone. Beyond, there is more water in an antique fountain; this is surrounded by four cypresses, providing vertical structure, with blue verbena at their feet, while the white trumpets of *Brugmansia arborea 'Knightii'* hang over tulbaghia and *Echium candicans*.

trees

Trees straddle the divide between hard structure and planting, playing a vital role both in the architecture and design of the garden and as living forms which grow and change with the seasons. It is important to choose the right size and shape to fit your garden. I so often come across shapeless trees that are too large for their allotted space and have to be pruned viciously.

We can learn a lot by observing trees in the countryside, where their volume gives rhythm and accentuates light, shade and contrast. In a garden they are the central structural element: as well as having ornamental value, they can be used to define spaces, enclose and frame, link, emphasize, enlarge or subdivide. They can act as a visual screen or a boundary. They may be needed for shade, to give height or to provide a windbreak. They link other features, and provide emphasis.

The choice of trees is influenced by the nature of the site as well as by practical considerations. In a broad landscape, it is best to use trees that are indigenous to the area. Trees with a natural form usually seem to work better in a soft landscape, while more angular trees work better in an urban setting or when used in a formal design. In smaller gardens, in general you should use small trees, though in some circumstances you can use one large tree to make a positive design statement. In either case, you must be sure to know the final size of the tree you choose. Narrow trees, such as cypresses or the larger *Quercus robur* f. *fastigiata,* are useful where space is limited.

My favourite small trees for the garden are *Crataegus persimilis* 'Prunifolia', the silver-leaved *C. laciniata* (syn. *C. orientalis*), *Acer aconitifolium*, all the stewartias and nearly all the crab apples, particularly *Malus* × *robusta* 'Red Sentinel', which keeps its red fruit all winter. All *Cornus kousa* and *C. florida* varieties can be of great ornamental value in small town gardens, particularly if seen from above. Ornamental cherries are good too.

In larger spaces, oak, lime and chestnut work well. I also like *Zelkova serrata*: with its distinctive tabular branch formation it creates a wonderful play of light and shade, and in autumn the leaves turn lovely shades of yellow and pink. *Sequoiadendron sempervirens* can look magnificent when planted in very large groups, their cinnamon-coloured trunks towering towards the sky.

Trees planted geometrically, in straight lines or at regular intervals, are useful tools for defining an area of the garden. For example, poplars, with their straight lines and white bark, become a very strong architectural feature when planted in formal rigid lines. I planted geometric lines of poplars in the watermeadows at Stanbridge Mill, and now after a few years the effect is wonderful – like a cathedral. Trees can also be placed to flank flights of steps or gateways or focus the eye towards a feature, be it the house or a vista. Traditionally, groups of trees of the same species were planted at regular intervals to line grand avenues. In the park at Eaton Hall in Cheshire I planted an avenue 550 metres (600 yards) long of horse chestnuts in eleven groups of eight, alternating white- and pink-blossomed trees. The avenue leads the eye from the Hall to a focus point – a series of grass rings of various heights.

On a more reduced scale, in a small country garden I achieved a similar effect by planting rows of *Crataegus persimilis* 'Prunifolia'.

The shape of a tree can form a pivotal part of the design. In Mediterranean countries, for example, where the strong landscape dictates tension, dark trees of linear, upright form, such as cypresses, are an interesting design tool. One pencil-like cypress planted on its own, not quite central in a circular or oval space, presents a strong contrasting image of peace and strength. A double row of cypresses might lead to a building, or direct the eye up a hill to a folly or point of view. When I think of cypress trees, my thoughts always turn to the long, formal avenue of Italian cypress (*Cupressus sempervirens* Stricta Group) at Bolgheri in the Maremma. The rows of cypress march up the hill for a kilometre, making a magnificent statement.

Left (detail) *Pinus pinea*
Below left Autumn tints glow like fire in a woodland setting at Gresgarth. Providing the flame among the green are *Cercidiphyllum japonicum, Cornus alternifolia, Acer japonicum, Malus toringoides* and *M. × zumi* 'Golden Hornet'.
Below A sparkling white scene at Gresgarth: the beautiful blossoms of *Prunus* 'Shirotae' are interspersed with the scented *Hamamelis × intermedia* 'Pallida' and underplanted with *Narcissus* 'Thalia' and *N.* 'Dove Wings'.

Generally, while upright trees are used for a more formal approach, broad, spreading trees look at their best in an informal design, or when they are used singly or in groups in a wider landscape setting. Planted as avenues they give a more natural, softer look. Olive trees, which in Mediterranean countries are traditionally planted in straight lines following the lie of the land, offer an exception to this rule. Their loose habit and gnarled shapes notwithstanding, they have a very definite design structure that lends itself to a formal architectural approach.

For a ribbon of trees marking a river meandering through a valley I would choose the spreading *Salix alba*, or *Populus candicans*, which looks like a silver cloud when the wind turns its leaves. Using trees in this way is a good way to give a strong identity to particular areas or spaces. You might, however, want to interrupt the monotony by planting groups of Lombardy poplars intermittently, thus creating a rhythm along the river.

When planting trees for posterity in a natural setting I generally allow enough space for each tree to reach its full potential, but if I want to use trees as a design tool to create a formal effect, then I plant them very close together in a geometric pattern. *Amelanchier canadensis* and *Acer davidii* (the snakebark maple) are both good for this type of planting, which works well near a building.

I also like to plant trees in circles, in order to enclose and surround an area: a circle of *Prunus* 'Taihaku' planted within a circular yew hedge with nothing else to distract the eye; or, alternatively, a circular copse, with the white-barked *Betula utilis* var. *jacquemontii* filling the space, surrounded by a tall double hedge to increase the sense of enclosure and tension.

Trees also make a design feature when planted in clumps, but only mix species in a group if you are planting a natural woodland; otherwise, simplicity is best. For flowers or autumn colour, I like to plant groups of the same species or cultivar. At Stanbridge Mill, in Dorset, I planted a large group of *B. u.* var. *jacquemonti* as a focal point to be seen in the distance from the house. The grass is cut just twice or three times a year, and the bluebells and wild flowers have been encouraged to establish. I would like to plant a large clump of *Acer griseum*, the paperbark maple, in this way. Though very slow-growing, this maple, with its cinnamon-coloured bark, looks wonderful in a mass, particularly in the autumn when the leaves turn red and scarlet.

Trees are usually left to grow in their natural shape, but they can be pruned to create different effects. I particularly like pleached trees – that is, trees grown with their branches severely pruned and entwined or interlaced so that they form a kind of hedge on stilts. The branches can either be trained on a ladder-like structure, with the side-shoots cut back every year to form a very narrow thick hedge, or they can be kept clipped to shape. Pleaching is a useful way of creating shade in a restricted space, as well as a powerful design tool. Because of their regular, geometric shapes, pleached trees have an immediate and recognizable identity. They give a strong sense of structure to the garden or avenue and create a play of light and shade. They also remain interesting in winter when the leafless branches form an eerie, sculptural, elegant shape.

Pleaching is a method much used in northern Europe, particularly in France and Belgium where you see it in both private and public spaces. The traditional choice of trees for pleaching is hornbeam or lime. At Reux a rectangular pool is emphasized by the pleached hornbeams that surround it. At Belvedere I used pleached limes to add height to the parterre and act as a transition between the garden and the tall trees on the side of the terrace,and at Eaton Hall, I created a link between the house and an existing church tower by planting pleached limes between the two. At Gresgarth, where pleached limes are planted as a walk at the end of the garden, they act as a windbreak, modifying the force of the fierce wind and providing shelter for the herbaceous borders nearby, as well as making a further, higher hedge above the yew hedges.

Horse chestnut and planes are also used extensively in France, Belgium, Italy and northern Europe, and *Quercus ilex*, the holm oak, is used mainly in Mediterranean countries. Clipped holm oaks played an important part in the design of both Roman and Renaissance gardens. Sadly, they seem to have fallen out of favour with garden designers, perhaps because they cast such a dense shade: this makes them wonderfully cooling to walk under, but means that nothing will grow underneath. Smaller trees suitable for pleaching include *Sorbus aria* , crab apples, pear trees and some crataegus, all good in smaller gardens, or for creating a more rural effect. In Barbados, where European trees cannot be used because of the tropical climate, I planted pleached *Ficus benjamina* to surround a formal garden. A perfect enclosure was established in three years. The problem now is to keep it in shape, for trees grow at great speed in the tropics.

Left In tropical gardens, the royal palm, *Roystonea regia*, is strikingly decorative and architectural.

Top right I love to use the soaring, pencil-like shapes of fastigiate cypresses as punctuation points and for vertical interest. In a Mediterranean garden, because they are native trees, they can be used, as here at Las Navas, to mark the boundary of a formal area and as a transition to a wilder, more naturalistic landscape beyond.

Middle right Sometimes, especially in a formal situation, I like to plant trees rising out of clipped topiary shapes, as in this avenue of apple trees in mounds of *Hebe subalpina*. This also protects the trees from being damaged by careless mowing.

Bottom right The gnarled shapes of pleached plane trees have a twisted beauty, and their large leaves are very decorative.

hedges

A hedge is an adaptable architectural tool, defining design or acting as a punctuation in a garden. It can be kept simple in form or cut to different heights, castellated or topped with balls or topiary shapes. Hedges can establish intimacy or unite different parts of the garden. Low hedges can divide areas of the garden while still allowing a feeling of openness. High hedges can enclose completely, or have windows cut into them to give views into the landscape. On a practical level, they provide protection from the wind and can also be used to hide unsightly areas.

Yew, which is compact and dark, makes a perfect hedge for a formal design. Box, being slow-growing, is mainly used for small hedges; however, given time, *Buxus sempervirens* will grow tall and wide and make a thick hedge, softer and more relaxed than yew, that will act as a good windbreak, as well as an attractive foil for deciduous plants. In Italy box is often used in preference to yew (which needs more water), and there are many large box hedges, some of them reaching up to 3 metres (10 feet).

Quercus ilex, the holm oak, is more open and lax in habit, and has larger dark green-grey leaves. In Italy it is often used to line large avenues or entrance courtyards. It grows fast and is quite tough – I have grown it at home in Lancashire, and it seems to thrive. It makes huge hedges, so it needs a lot of space.

Cupressus sempervirens, the Italian cypress, is fast-growing and clips well. A clipped cypress hedge is a wonderful architectural feature in a Mediterranean garden, and the dark green colour makes a marvellous background for statues as well as flowers. In a mild climate, *Pittosporum tobira*, dark-leaved and lax, with white, scented flowers in early summer, makes a good informal hedge. I have used it in Spanish gardens, including Las Navas.

If your design does not demand an evergreen structure but you need to define an area or create a vista, then a hornbeam or beech hedge makes a good choice. There is nothing prettier than a beech hedge in the spring when the new translucent leaves start to unfold. Like cypress, both beech and hornbeam will grow to a great height. In a damp garden, quick-growing alder will make a tall hedge very fast. Woven willow can also be used for hedges; in a wet area the willow can be planted directly into the ground, where it grows quickly.

You can plant hedges in juxtaposition to one another at varying heights, perhaps using different species to achieve a contrast of leaf colour, shape and texture. I like to use different hedging plants

Far left, top Hedges of cypress – *Cupressus sempervirens* – enclose the yellow garden at Las Navas, opening and closing the view to the distant fountain.

Left, top Round the sunken garden I designed in Barbados, I planted pleached *Ficus benjamina* to make a high-level hedge on stilts. A shingle-roofed pergola, partly covered with the jade vine (*Strongylodon macrobotrys*), crosses the garden, dividing it into four, and so the whole area is pleasantly shady.

Centre At Stanbridge Mill, the different textures and levels of a low box hedge edging a lawn, a double row of taller yew hedging hiding a path and, on higher ground, a beech hedge enclosing another garden room make a fascinating architectural juxtaposition.

Far left, bottom Underneath bright blossoms of *Rosa* 'New Dawn', buttresses of yew hedge beneath clipped *Pyrus salicifolia* 'Pendula' bring rhythm and formality to the planting against the moat walls at Château de Reux.

Left, bottom At Ascott House, I transformed a long straight walk between the front of the house and the lily pond by planting a serpentine beech hedge to make the route more dramatic and interesting.

together. At Stanbridge, for example, I planted four different hedges one above the other: a low box hedge encloses a square garden with a mound at the centre; a path runs along one side and is flanked by yew hedges; on higher ground, a beech hedge encloses a square garden; and above this, pleached limes enclose the garden at a higher level. From a distance the effect is of a green wall made of escalating hedges, with different textures and colours.

I associate tapestry hedges with cottage gardens; they can develop extraordinary patterns as the different coloured leaves weave into each other. They are planted in lengths, repeating the sequence of plants at intervals: beech, hawthorn, sometimes copper beech and holly can be used. For a more rustic look, a hedge could also contain ash, elder, may, blackthorn and wild roses.

Cut-and-laid farm hedges, the traditional hedges of the British countryside, are basket-like structures made up of plants like hawthorn, cornus, alder, blackthorn and wild roses. Their shape comes from the way that the branches are cut, bent and woven into each other. I always recommend cut-and-laid hedges for rural settings where there is no need for a formal statement: as well as making sturdy fences, they are good for wildlife.

When planting a hedge, I prefer to start with small plants: they have more time to become established, tend to be healthier, don't suffer from transplanting, and make a better hedge in the long term. Some designers and clients, however, prefer to use large, established plants, for an instant effect. When planting a yew hedge, make sure that all the plants are of the same cultivar, as sometimes a nursery's stock will include plants with different growing habits. Watch out for plants affected with phytophera, a fungus which attacks the roots: it is particularly liable to strike where the drainage is bad. There is an antidote, but it is not always effective.

Smaller hedges can be made of lavender or rosemary, and I often use these in Spain and Italy, as well as box and myrtle. I like to use rosemary as a delicate surround to a rose garden. Rose hedges can be made from Hybrid Musk roses, *Rosa rugosa*, *R. pimpinellifolia* or sweetbriar. They are all scented, and though they are too open to offer protection from winter wind, they are suitable to enclose an intimate garden. Santolinas and *Teucrium* × *lucidrys* also make good small hedges, so long as they have good drainage and do not have to cope with wet and freezing winters.

Left A wonderful contrast of colour, shape and texture, with clipped golden Irish yew, *Pyrus salicifolia* 'Pendula' and buttresses of dark green yew.
Right, top to bottom Solid dark blocks of yew provide a perfect frame for the white flowers of roses 'Iceberg' and 'Blanche Double de Coubert', *Crambe cordifolia* and white agapanthus. Box hedges snugly enclose and protect raised vegetable beds contained by hazel hurdles. I love the look of a pattern of hedging that rises in layers and projects at regular intervals like this stepped box hedge backed by walls and buttresses of yew.

PLANTING THE GARDEN

If the structural elements in the design of the garden are its flesh and bones, the planting is its clothing and the most immediately striking element. When planning the planting for a garden, I first observe the existing vegetation, and consider how best to use the species already growing on site. Because trees and hedges are so important in the structure of the garden, they have already been discussed in the section on structure (pages 44–51). Of course they are what I look at first. Sometimes some of the existing tree groupings need reinforcing to enhance the design. Sometimes new groupings are needed – to create enclosures or vistas, to extend or enhance the flowering season, or to introduce autumn colour or winter interest. Then I decide where hedges will be needed to create the necessary spaces and which species will be most suitable.

Above The distinction between a country garden and the landscape should not be too severe, so I like to use native plants, as I did with these parasol pines, *Pinus pinea*, at La Bandiera in the Maremma in Italy.
Right One of my favourite shrubs for autumn colour is *Viburnum plicatum* 'Grandiflorum'; it has a good architectural shape and at Gresgarth it never fails to produce fantastically red leaves in the autumn.

PLANTS FOR THE GARDEN

Once the trees and hedges have been decided I can concentrate on the other plants. The kinds of plants I particularly like to use are discussed below. This is not an exhaustive account, but a very personal selection of the plants I love best and those I have found to be most effective.

shrubs

As well as having enormous ornamental potential, shrubs can be used to link and define; to enclose and divide; to shelter and screen. They can also be employed as architectural features to provide form, texture or colour in conjunction with hard elements of the landscape in a naturalistic planting.

Because there is such an enormous variety of plants you will always be able to find the right shrub for even the most difficult situation, but at the same time the sheer quantity of species and cultivars available can make the whole process very difficult. So when you are choosing shrubs it is important to focus: it is useful to make a list of shrubs that are the correct size for your garden and that will also flower at different times of year.

Consider the habit of a particular shrub: one with a good architectural shape can be planted on its own, with only groundcover beneath. Although shrubs planted as background can be massed together, one planted on its own must have enough space around it to allow it to grow to its natural size, so it is important to find the right site. So often people plant shrubs in the wrong place: for example, I have seen, a *Parrotia persica* which, when naturally grown, has a wonderful open architectural shape, clipped because it had grown too large for the space; as a result it had completely lost its natural elegant form.

In a small garden a single shrub can make an interesting focal point: *Cornus controversa* 'Variegata', for example, is a wonderful eye-catcher and should be planted on its own; so should *Viburnum plicatum* 'Mariesii' with its striking layered effect, and *Magnolia sieboldii*, whose beautiful shape and white, pendulous, scented flowers look lovely when it is planted in a raised bed or behind a seat.

For a low-maintenance border, shrubs can be planted together in small groups close enough so that, when fully

grown, no bare ground will show beneath them, but with enough space to allow them to achieve their natural shape. The usual calculation is an average of one plant per square metre or square yard for large shrubs, and slightly closer together for smaller ones. If each shrub in the group is to have a separate identity, then they should be planted with slightly more space between them. To fill out the border while your chosen shrubs are growing, you can plant groundcover around them; alternatively, you can over-plant – that is, plant more shrubs than you will eventually need, removing the extraneous ones as your chosen shrubs grow into their full size. In some cases you might want to prune a shrub after a few years; if so, all the twiggy, lower growth should be removed, and a good architectural shape encouraged by completely removing old branches; this will also give you the opportunity to underplant below it.

You can grow almost any shrub in a pot, but, because the roots are constricted, it will never grow to its natural height. The soil should be improved every year and the plant must be fed and watered regularly. Among the most glamorous species to grow in a pot are camellias; they are tough and don't seem to mind the constriction – they still give a good show of flowers and are very decorative.

In open spaces the choice of shrubs should be kept simple. Depending on their size, choose just one or two varieties and plant them in big clumps; this will emphasize the design, and make a strong statement. If the open space is one that you drive through, you will need an even bigger grouping of each shrub in order to make an impression on the eye as you move more quickly through it.

Some shrubs, because of their compact, dense or architectural shapes, are particularly good for defining spaces. Box and yew are classic examples, but there are many shrubs that can be used for this effect – as punctuation or focal points, or to define or surround an area. Skimmias and hebes have an architectural rounded quality, rather like that of box, although skimmias and hebes are a little more relaxed in shape, and don't need clipping. *Skimmia* 'Kew Green', *S. laureola* and other cultivars have a naturally compact shape, as does the slightly larger *Hebe salicifolia*, with its white panicles of flowers. The grey *H. topiaria*, as its name suggests, makes a very tidy rounded shape, while *H. rakaiensis* with its fresh pale green, small, box-like leaves is more sprawling though still rounded. Some of the larger hollies have a very solid, permanent shape and can be used as architectural punctuation or on either side of a large entrance: *Ilex luscombensis* is particularly useful if you need an evergreen, narrow, upright shape. *Rosa pimpinellifolia*, with double yellow, white or pink blooms, provides a larger and deciduous round shape, pretty for an entrance in informal areas or as natural punctuation. Other shrubs such as *Cornus controversa* 'Variegata' have a very natural architectural shape.

A shrub should be used to make the most of its character – I wouldn't want to plant a deutzia, for instance, on the corner of a border or at an entrance because it is not a compact shape; it will look better in a more informal place mixed with other shrubs or planted at the back of the border.

As an example of using the natural shapes of shrubs and trees to make a design statement, I have just planned a woodland garden in an area which had no particular character. Within it I have designed a circular space – a glade – in which I will plant a circle of *Rhododendron williamsianum*, alternating between deep pink and pale pink flowering varieties. Behind the rhododendrons there will be a circle of *Magnolia loebneri* 'Merrill' which has highly scented large

white flowers and is very reliable; *Rhododendron william-sianum* is a very good, rounded shape and doesn't grow much more than 1.5 metres (5 feet) high; the leaf is neat and pretty – its young growth is bronze which turns to a handsome green. It looks very effective against the larger leaves of magnolias or of other, taller rhododendrons.

Even when used for shelter and screening, if they are well chosen shrubs can bring interest to the garden. Evergreen shrubs are always good as background, but I like it when they are mixed with lighter-leaved deciduous shrubs. It is fascinating to mix together varying shapes and shades of leaf with shrubs of different habits and flowering periods. If you have large masses of evergreen shrubs like holly or osmanthus, it relieves the monotony of the ubiquitous green to add some silver-leaved shrubs such as *Salix elaeagnos*, *Elaeagnus angustifolia* or *E. umbellata*, which has scented flowers, or *Cotoneaster franchetii*, which produces colourful berries in the autumn. Variegated shrubs have a similar lightening effect – for example, any of the variegated hollies or *Ligustrum ovalifolium* 'Argenteum', which is seldom seen but which I find very useful, hardy and pretty – as do bright or fresh green leaves such as those of *Griselinia littoralis*, for example, in more ornamental areas. *Weigela* 'Praecox Variegata' is a variegated small shrub which looks good with roses and herbaceous plants, and a planting combination I have recently found effective is *Cornus alternifolia* in a large border with nearby the smaller *Rhododendron* 'Alice Findlay' and *R. vaseyi*, with a group of *Mahonia* × *media* 'Charity' in the background.

Whenever space allows and I need to make a strong statement, I like to plant shrubs in large groups. At Gresgarth, for winter colour and to cheer me up, I have planted twenty different cultivars of hamamelis. I was inspired to do this after visiting the arboretum at Kalmthout in Belgium where many hamamelis have been bred and crossed. With flowers ranging from the palest yellow to bright yellow, orange and deep red, these plants are a real delight on a depressing winter's day.

I also love to use repetition. Along a path or stream, for example, I like to plant the whole length in repeating groups of azaleas, *Rhododendron luteum* alternating with *R.* 'Whitethroat' planted in double rows; if the distance is not long or if I need to make a really strong statement I will plant the same shrub all the way along.

Below, left to right *Cornus kousa* var. *chinensis*, seen here in full flower at Gresgarth, and, to the left, *C. k.* 'Satomi' are both beautifully shaped ornamental shrubs. *Cornus controversa* 'Variegata' stretches its horizontal branches over tulips, pulmonaria and pale yellow primulas in the spring border at Ascott The huge waving fan-shaped leaves of *Livingstonia chinensis* contribute structure and movement to a border in the Barbados garden. Clusters of red berries follow on from the flowers of *Viburnum opulus* 'Notcutt's Variety' – seen here with the remaining autumn leaves of *Nyssa sylvatica* above and *Cotoneaster atropurpureus* 'Variegatus' below – making it decorative throughout the year. An ornate Coalbrookdale iron seat nestles among shrubs in a border that includes *Rosa* 'Charles Austin', *Symphoricarpos orbiculatus* 'Foliis Variegatiis', *Delphinium* 'Faust' and *Ruta graveolens* 'Jackman's Blue'. *Rhododendron williamsianum* with dark auriculas in a woodland spring border at Eaton Hall.

Pages 56–7, clockwise from top left A lovely – but un-named – pink rhododendron in a woodland planting at Gresgarth, behind *Persicaria affinis* 'Superba' and buttercups in long grass. The scented yellow azalea *Rhododendron luteum*, with *Tulipa* 'Helmar', in a spring planting at Gresgarth. An architectural Mediterranean planting on the blue terrace at La Bandiera: olives with their silvery foliage and *Melianthus major* with its striking leaves and dark brown flower spikes, over low-growing plants such as daisy-like *Erigeron karvinskianus* and creeping *Convolvulus sabatius*. The beautiful salmon-pink trumpets and large leaves of *Brugmansia* × *candida* 'Blush' in a tropical planting in Barbados, against the equally striking leaves of caladiums, variegated *Crinum asiaticum* var. *japonicum* and *Murraya paniculata*.

Roses are my very favourite plants, as of course they are for so many people. I like their habit, soft, romantic and yielding, their colours, their scent; to me they are the epitome of an English garden, and I plant them in profusion, particularly old-fashioned roses.

The rose family is so large and can be used effectively in so many different ways. Roses can ramble and sprawl, they can be grown as bushes or clipped as a hedge, used as low-growing groundcover or as climbers over pergolas, up walls and into trees. But their drawback is that for so many months of the year many of the best roses have no flowers and don't look particularly attractive. For this reason, if space allows, when planting borders I mix roses with other plants – rosemary, lavender, santolina and shrubs such as choysia, deutzia, philadelphus or *Cotinus coggygria* Rubrifolius Group. To extend the flowering season in the rose garden I like to include herbaceous plants like campanulas or iris and bulbs to flower at other times of the year, as well as repeat-flowering roses such as Hybrid Musks and Floribundas.

For practicality I particularly love Hybrid Musk roses. Not only are they repeat-flowering, they are also tough and disease-free, and on the whole they are very reliable, and easy to prune. If I am designing a garden where the climate is difficult – particularly where it is wet – I always choose Hybrid Musks because, as well as coming in wonderful colours, they withstand a variety of conditions. I am never without them, and in fact I don't think there's a single scheme that I have designed where I haven't planted them somewhere.

I do of course have my favourites: among these are 'Buff Beauty', 'Felicia' – which flowers well into the winter – 'Penelope', and 'Wilhelm'. I like to mix 'Buff Beauty' with blue herbaceous plants like *Nepeta racemosa* 'Walker's Low' or *Aconitum* 'Spark's Variety', and to have a dark burgundy clematis such as 'Rouge Cardinal' scrambling through it, or to combine the buff flowers with the delicate tawny grasses *Deschampsia cespitosa* 'Goldtau' or *Molinia caerulea* subsp. *arundinacea*. I tend to plant 'Felicia' and 'Penelope' in large groups, and I think that the deep red 'Wilhelm' is good when

Above left I have found that many of the pretty modern English roses do best in warm, dry conditions. In the right climate, as here at Las Navas in Spain, *Rosa* 'Graham Thomas' keeps its bushy shape and flowers until late in the year.
Below left At Ascott House I filled two borders with a mass of old-fashioned roses like 'Empress Josephine', 'Souvenir de la Malmaison' and 'William Lobb', seen here with companion planting of white and blue *Campanula lactiflora* and *Nepeta* 'Six Hills Giant'.

Above right At Eaton Hall, the shrub rose *Rosa xanthina* 'Canary Bird' looks very graceful trained as a standard, its flowers echoed in a minor scale by the potentilla at its feet.
Below right At Little Malvern Court, a garden I designed some time ago, great mounds of roses, including 'Tuscany Superb' and 'Zigeunerknabe' ('Gipsy Boy') and soft groundcover spill over and soften the lines of the stone paving.

planted with the pink 'Felicia'. Hybrid Musk roses are tidy plants and can also be pruned to form a hedge, for example surrounding a meadow or a rose garden; this encloses the area without changing the informal feeling of the place.

I am passionate about all the old-fashioned roses, especially the most difficult one of all, 'Souvenir de la Malmaison', which comes as a shrub and a climber. Unfortunately it doesn't like me, or the climate where I live in north-west England, for it hates the rain and balls up at the faintest drop. *Rosa gallica* is relatively easy because it is quite sturdy and does not need support. *R. g.* 'Versicolor' (Rosa Mundi) should always be planted in a row or a large clump: the wonderful bicoloured pink and burgundy of the flowers is much more effective *en masse*. I particularly like it along a narrow path or as a hedge in a herb garden.

I also like planting big clumps of *R.* 'Complicata' or any of the species roses in a wild meadow because they look natural and romantic, and have wonderful scent and lax growth. Another favourite is the Scotch rose, *R. pimpinellifolia*; it flowers early and has a pleasing rounded shape. A true country rose, it comes in both single and double forms, making a thick thorny thicket, and can be pink, yellow or white. It is very fragrant; I have a nameless pink form which was given to me, and when it is in flower the most wonderful scent wafts into the house. These roses look very well at the end of a long walk; they make an excellent hedge, and are also pretty as specimen shrubs in long grass. They flower very early in the summer, and they have a lovely, simple look.

Bourbon roses have beautiful flowers, with marvellous shape and scent. They flower particularly well – and look neat and tidy – when trained over a vertical structure. A wigwam of hazel provides a good support, and the frame, which looks like a basket, is attractive in the winter; metal hoops or wooden trellised structures are also suitable and can be decorative if well made. Old-fashioned roses can also do well when four or five are planted together in mown lawn or long grass, supported by a square wooden frame; when the roses are in flower, they will cascade to the ground.

Clockwise from top left The pale tones of the Hybrid Musk *Rosa* 'Buff Beauty' are perfectly set off by the dark *Clematis* 'Rouge Cardinal' threading through it. I use *Rosa* 'Iceberg' and its climbing form, shown here grown on a pyramid, all the time in warm, dry climates because it produces masses of its pretty shining white clusters of flowers so reliably. Another favourite is the old-fashioned rose 'William Lobb', which I have planted at Gresgarth trained on a metal support so that its scented flowers can hang down gracefully. The exquisitely pretty pink blooms of *R.* 'Fritz Nobis' growing through long grass and meadow flowers.

Roses can also be planted for their hips, which come in many different sizes and in colours from bright red to black and are very good for cutting for the house. I particularly like *R. roxburghii*, which has hips covered in stiff prickles.

Hybrid Tea roses are difficult to grow and to place in the garden – they are so delicate and such an ugly shape, particularly in winter. I grow them only for cutting: I love huge bowls filled with them in every colour, the stalks cut very short so that they form a cushion. But I recommend the old varieties of Hybrid Tea, not the modern ones, which tend to have no scent.

There are so many climbers to choose from. The Banksian rose is one of my favourites. I have often seen it climbing up the façades of palaces in Rome, and if you walk down the Spanish Steps you see terrace after terrace of *R. banksiae* entwined with *Wisteria sinensis*. On a trip to Syria twenty years ago, we saw the famous waterwheels of Hamah covered in yellow *R. banksiae* and surrounded by fields of wildflowers, *Artemisia arborescens* and iris. (We went back this year and all this had gone; the river was dry, there were no roses and the meadows were covered in concrete.) When I need to cover a large wall, I will nearly always plant Banksian roses – particularly *R. banksiae* 'Lutea'. I also like *R.* 'Gloire de Dijon', which has beautifully full, warm buff flowers, repeats later in the season, and looks wonderful next to the small flowers of the Banksian rose. *R.* 'Madame Grégoire Staechelin' is another good early flowerer, though not the easiest.

On the whole, roses need open spaces with good air circulation and fertile clay soil. When planning a rose garden, it is important to ensure that the beds are large enough to allow adequate space between the roses. In areas where the rainfall is high, or the soil thin, the only roses that really thrive are some of the species and most of the old-fashioned roses. These are often tougher than other types, such as the new English roses – which actually revel in warmer climates and in rich soil. For example, I have planted quantities of the modern English rose *R.* 'Graham Thomas' at Las Navas in Spain where they are a great success, flowering throughout the summer until Christmas, without ever getting leggy; in Lancashire, on the other hand, where the rain leeches the soil of nutrients, I have had to take it out because it looks so lanky and unhappy. Even Floribundas do not do particularly well in my local climate, not even *R.* 'Iceberg', my favourite standby, which never stops flowering in Italy, Greece and Spain. 'Iceberg' is often unfairly despised, because it is used so widely, but where it likes the climate it is highly reliable, produces its lovely white flowers continuously and is an asset in any garden.

I use clematis a lot, both in my garden designs and at Gresgarth. They are wonderfully varied: some are scented, some have wonderful seed heads and others are so large that they can reach the top of a tree; and you can have a different variety in flower in almost every month of the year. I particularly like the species clematis and the smaller-flowered varieties, including *Clematis macropetala* and *C. alpina* in the spring and the Viticellas in the autumn. My earliest favourite is *C. cirrhosa* var. *balearica*, which has beautiful foliage and flowers in late winter, followed by the macropetalas and alpinas. The montanas and 'Spooneri' flower just before the large-flowered varieties, which in turn are followed by the viticellas and the late-flowerers, such as *C. tangutica* with its yellow paper-lantern-like flowers followed by silky-tasselled seed heads, the lovely 'Bill MacKenzie' and cowslip-scented *C. redheriana*.

I am specially fond of the deep blue *C.* 'Perle d'Azur', which is utterly reliable and never fails to look wonderful. I also like *C.* 'Betty Corning', which is small with delicate pale grey-blue flowers and *C.* 'Alba Luxurians' which has white flowers tipped with green, with almost black stamens; this is good for planting to scramble over and through shrub roses, as are also the earlier alpinas and macropetalas.

Herbaceous clematis are useful for filling gaps in the border when other flowers are over. Those that I like include *C. recta* 'Purpurea', which has dark purple leaves and a mass of white flowers, and *C. jouiniana* 'Praecox', with small, pale lilac flowers – this is very attractive grown over a stump or through a shrub. *C.* × *eriostemon* 'Hendersonii' is a good variety which can also climb through shrubs. Of the newer clematis I like *C.* 'Moonbeam', which is covered in starry white flowers in early spring, and the short-growing *C.* 'Arabella', with pale blue flowers over a long period.

Ivy is a marvellous foil for other plants, and in particular for other climbers. My husband planted it on the wall opposite our small house in London. The wall is close and as high as the house itself, which made it daunting and ugly when it was bare. After a few years the wall was completely covered with *Hedera helix*. In front of it is planted *Wisteria floribunda* 'Multijuga', which has panicles of blue flowers 60 centimetres (2 feet) long. This now stands proud of the ivy, and looks fantastic against the dark green background. This planting is demanding, for once a year, in the early spring, the ivy has to be clipped right back so that it is flush to the wall. This stops it getting out of hand. *Hedera helix* can be a very damaging and invasive climber; I have seen this in Italy where removing it from a building brought down much of the stucco as well, so I do not plant it often. There are, however, many different species of ivy and not all of them are as destructive. They come in different textures, leaf sizes and colour variegation as well as different degrees of tenacity.

Another good climber with tendrils is *Hydrangea anomala* subsp. *petiolaris*. I like to plant it *en masse* – a long wall completely covered with it looks spectacular. It thrives in shade, is extremely decorative when in flower and looks interesting in the winter because of the branch formation. Again, it must be watched for, once established, it can become rampant. I sometimes plant it to grow up trees, which is its natural habit. *H. seemannii* is another vigorous climber and would also, in the wild, scramble over bushes and into trees. They are both very good groundcoverers as well, forming huge mounds. *Schizophragma hydrangeoides* is a very ornamental climber, most effective on a wall and good in shade. It is a little like *Hydrangea anomala* subsp. *petiolaris*, but the flowers are prettier and more elegant. There is a larger species, *Schizophragma integrifolium*, which has even better flowers and leaves but this prefers a sunny wall.

Honeysuckles are such charming climbers and there are so many to choose from. Two I like are *Lonicera periclymenum* and *L. tragophylla*. *L. periclymenum* 'Munster' seems to be less rampant and more manageable than others; I planted it to grow over the side edge of a flight of steps, and it keeps to its place like a little hedge. *L. tragophylla* is shade-loving and perfect for a dull corner where it will flower in early summer; its long, golden yellow flowers are very exotic. I must add to the list *L. hildebrandiana*, the giant honeysuckle, which in the wilds of its native Burma reaches the top of huge trees. It has leaves 7–15 centimetres (3–6 inches) long, and the scented flowers can be 10 centimetres (4 inches) across. I grow it in my greenhouse and bring it into the house when it is in flower.

An excellent semi-evergreen climber is *Akebia trifoliata*. I like it for its fragrant dark purple flowers, drooping in racemes in spring. I use *Actinidia kolomikta* sparingly because, although its leaves tipped with white and pink are attractive, it can look rather garish if it is planted in the wrong place.

When I want a climber with big leaves I almost always plant

On a terrace outside the guest house at Las Navas in Spain, the climbing roses 'Guinée' and 'Madame Grégoire Staechelin' intertwine to make a stunning display on an iron pergola which I designed in the Moorish style. Solid platforms of box at the four corners visually anchor the towering arch of roses.

Vitis coignetiae, which is so architectural; the silhouette of the leaves when framing a view or a window is very striking. I also use *Ampelopsis henryana* for its wonderfully shaped dark green or bronze leaves with silvery white variegation, particularly good when growing in half-shade; they turn red in the autumn. Also good for autumn colour are *Vitis* 'Brant' and *Celastrus orbiculatus,* both of whose leaves turn golden yellow.

Good evergreens are *Holboellia,* with glossy green leaves, which is especially useful for walls with ugly drainpipes, and *Trachelospermum jasminoides,* whose white flowers are scented in warmer climates; this is a good climber for town gardens and is useful for twining without clinging. Suited for shady or rather dismal areas is *Pileostegia viburnoides.* This

beautiful evergreen has leathery, long, elegantly pointed leaves; large ligustrum-like panicles of flowers appear late in the summer. I planted one to grow on a shady, rather dank wall where the planting bed had to be very small. I have been surprised to see how well it has grown and how decorative it is.

The most spectacular climber for the tropics is *Strongylodon macrobotrys* (the jade vine). This has incredible flowering panicles up to 1 metre (3 feet) in length, carrying many flowers over a long period. It looks wonderful grown over an open pergola so that the flowers can hang down through the struts. Although not as vigorous as the jade vine, another tropical climber, *Thunbergia mysorensis,* is also best grown over a pergola so that its pendulous orange flowers can be viewed from below. This thunbergia prefers a shady part of the garden. In the tropics you can cut it down to nothing in mid-spring and by the autumn it has grown to its full height.

There are many different passionflower (*Passiflora*) species and cultivars which are interesting to grow, but they seem to exhaust themselves and, in my experience, usually have a short life in the tropics. However, I have grown the spectacular *P. quadrangularis* in a pot in my greenhouse, with great success. *Mucuna bennettii* is a splendid, huge woody climber introduced from New Guinea. It needs a large space, so it is not very good for small gardens. Another interesting tropical plant is *Beaumontia grandiflora*, a woody climber with large cup-shaped, fragrant white flowers. It must be grown against a house or over a very strong support, as must *Solandra grandiflora*, which has enormous pale yellow trumpets (sadly, without scent). It is a fast grower and after only two years it develops aerial roots which hang down from the shoots like a curtain. Perhaps the prettiest of all is *Petrea volubilis*, a rather slow grower, good for a confined space. It flowers after heavy rains, bearing panicles of a wonderful dark purple-blue; there is also a pure white form.

I love the waxy white flowers and glossy leaves of stephanotis, but I have not yet grown it successfully in the garden. It likes acid soil and it did not thrive at all in Barbados, even though I had changed the alkaline soil.

It is always important to decide whether you want an area to be covered by one climber, or more. Many roses, for example, only flower once, so you might want to add another, later-flowering rose or other climber. Remember, though, that while different colours of the same type of climber are effective, it is harder work to mix different species: for example, when roses and clematis are mixed together, unless you are careful to choose the right cultivars, the ensuing pruning programme can become complicated. However, roses are such a perfect foil for clematis that the effort is well worthwhile. In my opinion it is unwise to combine two twining rampant climbers, such as a wisteria and a rose, as they will be impossible to disentangle and will always look messy.

If you want to grow a variety of climbers, think about having a pergola. Where the setting is informal, you can clothe the pergola with roses and sweet peas. In a vegetable garden apples or pears, blackberries and the smaller gourds can be trained over a pergola. When using roses I often like to repeat a particular one at regular intervals, as this gives a stronger, more architectural feeling to the design. For one of my projects I designed a very long pergola which I painted black. I covered it with climbing roses of all different varieties and shades of red, but repeated *Rosa* 'American Pillar' at intervals all the way along the length; this unified the planting, giving it rhythm and continuity.

Climbers often look their best growing, as nature intended, through other plants as support. Here, the tendrils of a rosy-pink passionflower (*Passiflora vitifolia*) hang down gently from its host olive tree to caress the mauve spikes of *Lavandula dentata* growing beneath.

Wisteria tends to look best where you can appreciate the beauty of its dangling racemes, for example planted on a pergola. The white flowers of *Wisteria floribunda* 'Alba' show particularly well against the black of this painted wooden pergola. Their pointed, conical shape is contrasted with the round form of *Hebe subalpina* and the colour is echoed by *Iris sibirica* 'White Swirl'.

The neat, dark form of a fastigiate cypress standing sentinel by a steel sculpture in my Chelsea 2000 garden is charmingly decorated by the pale flowers of *Rosa* 'Climbing Lady Hillingdon' scrambling up it.

Bottom left The gracefully shaped, rich blue flowers of *Thunbergia grandiflora*, shining like stars against the backing of its luxuriant green leaves, cover a long pergola in a Mediterranean garden. This frames the view from a blue-painted Moorish seat overhung with *Brugmansia arborea* 'Knightii', set at the edge of a patio intricately patterned with stone and pebbles.

Clockwise from top left An arch covered in *Vitis* 'Brant' encloses a seat I designed for Ascott House. In a tiny London garden we covered a high wall with ivy and in front of it grew a *Wisteria floribunda* 'Multijuga': the wisteria's 60-centimetre (2-foot) long flower racemes glow against the dark background climber. The claw-like flowers of the jade vine (*Strongylodon macrobotrys*). *Clematis* 'Frances Rivis' decoratively climbing through a later-flowering rose. *Allamanda blanchetii* in front of *Pseuderanthemum atropurpureum* 'Variegatum'. *Rosa banksiae* 'Lutea' and *Wisteria sinensis* smother the front of this small London house.

herbaceous plants and bulbs

As a general rule, I would always want to choose the herbaceous plants that will thrive in the area where I am gardening. But of course I have my particular favourites that I use again and again, either because I have found them reliable or because they fulfil my design intentions. I am never without *Euphorbia schillingii*, *Campanula latifolia* and *C. lactiflora*, centranthus, phlomis, achillea and of course all the phlox, early and late.

I try to avoid planting herbaceous plants in a shrubbery, as – with such obvious exceptions as foxgloves, *Epilobium angustifolium* var. *album* and libertias – they tend to look untidy and unnatural. I do, however, like to plant a few shrubs in a herbaceous border if there is space: for example, *Cotinus coggygria* 'Royal Purple' will give depth to a pink or a blue/mauve border, while a silver shrub like *Elaeagnus angustifolia* Caspica Group is invaluable when you need a lighter effect. I always like to mix perennials with shrubs near the house, because this area needs to look good and have as much as possible in flower all the year round. Anyway, you always want to have as many as possible of your favourite plants next to the house. In these borders, as well as roses, philadelphus, *Viburnum farreri* 'Candissimum' and *Sarcococca humilis,* I like to have hellebores, herbaceous peonies, phlox, *Iris pallida*, lavender, santolina and rosemary.

Bulbs play an important part in gardens; they come into bloom over such a long season, and many of them flower at a time when nothing else is happening. Think of the snowdrop, which in some gardens starts flowering in midwinter, and the colchicums and autumn crocuses which flower up to the end of autumn.

If you are using bulbs in a natural environment you have to be very generous with them: great swathes of bulbs look more natural and impressive. If you are planting bulbs in borders, remember that they look untidy after flowering so should always be planted through or near a plant that will grow after the bulb has flowered and hide the messy, dying leaves. Small

A vibrant display of reds from *Tulipa* 'Attila' and *Erysimum cheiri* 'Vulcan'. The combination of hues is interesting and quite powerful, with the tulips a blue-red and the wallflowers a red with plenty of orange.

bulbs in borders should look as natural as possible; there is very little else in leaf early in the year and you should therefore be lavish in the planting.

Planting daffodils of different colours together looks unnatural. It is better to choose one colour and plant it generously – always throwing the bulbs on to the ground and planting them where they fall for a natural effect. It is worth finding out which narcissi or daffodil naturalize best in your area. I prefer white narcissi or pale daffodils and I do not like the ones with very large cups. My very favourite is 'Thalia', but it has proved to be extremely delicate, which is sad, and I am now trying other small white ones to see if they are more reliable. I never plant large daffodils or narcissi in borders because their leaves are unmanageable after flowering, but I like planting the smaller jonquil or narcissi – usually in tight clumps. I like to plant *Narcissus* 'Hawera', *N. triandrus* var. *triandrus* and *N.* 'February Silver' next to peonies, hellebores or hostas, which will hide their foliage after flowering.

Tulips are spectacular in borders, but are an expensive treat. You have to plant them every year, and then lift them after flowering; it is a lot of work but they do look wonderful planted in clumps or drifts and they have a terrific impact. In some gardens I have planted, in long grass, tulips which have been previously used for bedding out; this can look very pretty but it is a time-consuming exercise as they will only flower for a year or two and will hardly ever naturalize.

Tulips look good in a wildflower meadow, together with narcissi and *Anemone blanda*. The best anemone is the wood anemone, *A. nemorosa*, and it naturalizes easily. It is an

indicator of very old woodland and looks absolutely spectacular in the early spring with its white starry flowers carpeting the area it has colonized.

In sunny sites I use alliums and lilies – as many as possible, particularly *Lilium regale* and the oriental hybrids. In country garden borders and under trees I like *Cyclamen coum* and *C. hederifolium* and drifts of small crocuses like *Crocus tommasianus*. Camassias look at their finest in long grass or as part of a naturalistic planting. They like damp conditions, particularly *Camassia quamash*, which is smaller and more delicate than the others. In a mixed or herbaceous border camassias should be planted behind another herbaceous plant so that the leaves can be well hidden, as they last a long time and can look untidy; in long grass this does not matter. *C. leichtlinii* is excellent planted in

herbaceous borders because it flowers quite early, adding interest early on in the year. The flowers will soon be hidden below the rising herbaceous plants.

Below, far left I love to see small-flowered, pale daffodils naturalized in grass. At Gresgarth, the blossoms of *Prunus* 'Shirotae', with *P. yedoensis* in the background, hang gracefully over a sparkling white swathe of *Narcissus* 'Thalia' – my favourite narcissus – *N.* 'Jenny' and *N.* 'Dove Wings'.
Below middle A fresh spring planting of variegated pink tulips with pansies.
Below right The rich colours of *Tulipa* 'Helmar' rise through a background of the white-edged leaves of *Hosta undulata* var. *albomarginata*, with pale pink *Rhododendron* 'Amethystinum' behind.

PLANNING THE PLANTING

When planning the planting of your beds and borders there are so many things that must be considered, starting from the qualities of particular plants – their preferred habitat, their size, form and texture – through colour schemes and seasonal changes, to overall considerations of shape, proportion and scale. To make an impact in a garden you must plant in quantity, contrasting and complementing leaf shapes and colours. Furthermore, a garden is a living, changing entity, and

to avoid ossification the gardener should experiment with new planting ideas and different plant positions, whilst still attempting to maintain a structured design – not an easy balance to achieve.

Habitat and conditions

Good planting is dependent on understanding the unique character of each plant, and where it occurs naturally. Consider the simple example of the hosta: the natural habitat of the hosta is a spacious, shaded area which does not dry out where it will naturally grow into its given shape and size. If, however, it is planted in full sun, it will shrivel and look miserable. It is vital to select those plants that will flourish in the conditions of the particular site.

When planning the planting scheme for a garden one of the first considerations is to discover the pH of the soil – that is, its level of acidity or alkalinity. I don't think that it is practical, even if sometimes of interest, to grow plants that do not suit the particular soil pH of the garden. Changing the make-up of the soil is a short-lived solution, which invariably leads to maintenance problems.

Form and texture

Plants are three dimensional and their forms can often be used as sculptural elements in a garden, especially if their outline is well-defined or striking. Even the shadow or reflection of a particular plant on a wall or on water can become of as much aesthetic importance as the plant itself. Plants have almost limitless textural qualities – not simply the leaves and flowers, but also the bark and twigs – and they can be used to complement and contrast with each other. A dramatic, bold texture throws the plant into prominence, whilst a fine-textured plant will blend or retreat and suggest a sense of distance.

At Gresgarth, for example, I use the bold, exotic outline of the giant rhubarb (*Rheum palmatum*), planted in clumps at the water's edge. In spring the new growth is bright red with a tinge of orange, starting with a bright, fist-like shape which unfolds slowly into huge leaves. In the early stages the stems and leaves keep their striking colour and are a real eye-catcher when reflected in the water. I have also planted nearby a large group of *Rubus thibetanus*; their snowy, bare white stems rise through hellebores and the red young growth of herbaceous peonies. Excellent in a spring border, the rubus also combines prettily with roses, and the texture of its small silvery leaves give it an ethereal look.

For the small garden, the elegant branching and feathery-textured leaves of the smaller acers are very useful. *Acer palmatum* and *A. japonicum* are attractive in many ways, for they have beautiful trunks, in colours from green to cinnamon red. Some have white striations, and all have brilliant autumn colour, ranging from dark red to bright yellow. It is wonderful to sit under *A. japonicum* 'Aconitifolium' and look up through its pretty leaves. *A. palmatum* 'Seiryû' is one of my favourite small trees because not only is it amazingly tough (I have it in the coldest, windiest part of my garden at Gresgarth) but it colours beautifully in the autumn and looks enchanting in spring. Its bark is pale green and the small leaves are very finely dissected. This is good tree to plant near a window so that you can look through the delicate leaves.

Proportion and scale

Scale is an essential element of good design. It can be used to create an illusion of space where none exists, and is particularly useful in a smaller garden, where the use of small-scale trees and planting can make the garden and house seem large in comparison. Conversely, a large external space can be scaled down by using planting to readjust the proportions – with features like small woodlands and avenues used in such a way that the proportions are in harmony. At Eaton Hall the success of the borders I designed is largely due to the fact that they on a very large scale which means that they are in proportion with the imposing architecture of the Victorian terraces. However, a large plant can often have a dramatic effect in a small space – though the converse is never true.

Left, above This shady garden makes a good setting for *Hosta* 'Sum and Substance', its architectural leaves forming graphic shapes along a straight-edged grass path.
Left, below The enormous young leaves of the giant rhubarb (*Rheum palmatum*) make a dramatic display against the smooth lawn and tranquil lake at Gresgarth.
Right, above Complementary colours and textures create a pleasing effect in a border at La Bandiera. The glaucous, architectural leaves of *Cynara cardunculus* arch over the low-growing, feathery foliage of *Artemisia* 'Powis Castle'. The blue-green tones of all the foliage sets off to perfection the pinks of verbena and *Rosa* 'Heritage'.
Right below The fronds of *Sasa palmetto* spread like a mist above its strap-shaped leaves and below the ferny foliage of *Roystonea regia*.

colour and contrast

Colours and colour themes are important for the identity of a garden. If all colours were to be used, mixed, everywhere in the garden, there would be no harmony, no unity and no character. I try to use colour with care, to create an appropriate atmosphere and setting. For example, surrounding the entrance to a house I often use white and green; these colours are formal and neutral, setting off and not competing with the house. Around the terrace, I like to have a unified scheme, using perhaps mauvey-blue colours with a touch of pink, or pale pink and white, or a careful mix of colours that blend in together, with topiary and other evergreen shapes to make sure it looks good all year round. Not too far from the house could be a spring garden, all white, fresh and pretty, perhaps with *Prunus* 'Shirotae', white azaleas, primulas and pulmonarias. Elsewhere there could be a hot border of reds, oranges and yellows, or a border devoted to one colour but with mixed shades. Contrast is important too. I always like to oppose the excitement of a busy colourful border with a space, perhaps enclosed, of calm and no colour other than green.

A colour palette in a garden should preferably come from one colour base: you would not, for example, use an electric blue with a purple blue, or an orange pink with a mauvey pink. Reds and oranges are striking, while the paler colours are more soothing. I keep the reds and oranges on their own unless a border needs lifting, in which case I might add a touch of orange or red if I feel it needs it. It is in fact just like painting a picture. Of course, one mustn't forget when planting borders that the colour is only there for a short while – so you must try and think of it over a whole season – hence the complexity of the task.

Colour in planting should always be used in a positive way: plants with strong, eye-catching colours, for example, are best used in positions in full sun where their dominance can be emphasized and appreciated. The colour of some plants is so striking that it is very difficult to mix them with other shades. The blue of *Meconopsis grandis*, for example, is so dramatic, almost unearthly, that it is almost impossible to mix it with other blues; ideally I would combine meconopsis only with white candelabra primula and ferns. Equally I feel that the red dahlia 'Bishop of Llandaff' should not be combined with other reds; I would prefer to plant it in a large clump together with *Selinum tenuifolium*, which has very frothy white flowers, and the dark leaves of *Angelica atropurpurea* and *Atriplex hortensis* var. *rubra*, and small-flowered asters (Michaelmas daisies). Another mix I like is red Goliath Group poppies with *Heuchera* 'Palace Purple'.

Blue and white gives an air of distance, while orange and red become prominent and seem to come closer. Gertrude Jekyll, who was renowned for her use of colour, would often plant the warm colours near to hand, with blue and violet tones at the far end of a border, thus making the border seem longer. Generally, the colours of the plants seem to become stronger as the season progresses. Think of the pale spring yellow of aconites and new spring leaves compared to the hot russets of late summer.

I prefer not to mix contrasting colours, preferring tonal, complementary shades. Some palettes are more harmonious than others: orange and blue can be mixed, for example, as can orange and red – but not red and pink. Although contrasts are important and interesting in garden design, colour need not always be used in this way. Sometimes a plant will look better grown in a single, bold clump of one colour. Flamboyant colours, like those found in many varieties of rhododendron and azalea, should be grouped in single colour varieties, the colour softened with plants in subtler tones between the groups. Where there is a background of evergreens, the foreground colour must be chosen with great care. Red, for example, is too strong a contrast against such a dark background.

I don't like mixing very bright pink flowers with too much greenery; to my eye the contrast is too strong and I prefer to introduce some silver-leaved shrubs to lighten the tone. I have

Above A harmonious pink border at Eaton Hall, with *Geranium psilostemon*, *Delphinium* 'Ruby', *Rosa* 'Mevrouw Nathalie Nypels', *Stachys byzantina*, *Phlomis italica*, *Campanula latifolia* var. *alba*, pink scabious and pink lavender.
Opposite, clockwise from top left Orange *Iris* 'Radiant Summit' with purple *I.* 'Blue Sapphire'. Burgundy hyacinth 'Distinction' with *Euphorbia dulcis* 'Chameleon'. Shades of pink: *Papaver* 'Patty's Plum' and *Allium* 'Purple Sensation'. Pale pink *Iris* 'Beverly Sills' against purple *I.* 'Pagan Royal'. Fresh green *Alocasia macrorrhiza* and variegated *Gratophyllum pictum*. Black-purple *Tulipa* 'Negrita' against pale wallflowers.

also found that when – by mistake – I planted pink with orange, it looked wonderful. I prefer pale to bright pink generally, particularly a pink that has a little bit of mauve in it, and I always like to mix it with deep burgundy flowers and dark burgundy leaves; I never plant pink and blue together – it reminds me of nursery colours. I like different shades of pink which are not too sweet. Darker pinks like paler pinks mixed with them; in general a scarlet red like that of *Lychnis chalcedonica* does not go well with a pink-toned flower, while a touch of pink in orange and russet does very well. Red does, however, go well with pale blues and mauves – blue muscari with red tulips, for example.

Green flowers are very important in a garden, because they are attractive and mix well with any other colour; they are particularly good with white and with leaves in other greens; in fact a green and white border is a very refreshing sight. A green border needn't be dull because there are so many different leaf shapes and hues and variegations in the leaves. Some greens are blue, some are yellow, some have white streaks – some evergreens are duller greens and some are fresh greens. Green plants that I particularly like include euphorbias such as *Euphorbia sikkimensis, E. schillingii, E. mellifera* and *E. cornigera, Bupleurum fruticosum, Helleborus argutifolius* and *Angelica archangelica*. There is also *Nicotiana langsdorffii*, and *Alchemilla mollis* and of course ferns and hostas – and a very pretty wall shrub, *Itea ilicifolia*, which has long green tassels.

Blue and mauve and purple are my favourite colours; I think they are wonderfully cool and soothing. Blue looks good mixed with grasses, and particularly so with lemony greens. In warm temperate gardens you can use plants such as lavenders which you couldn't grow in the colder parts of Britain: *Lavandula*

latifolia, L. lanata, L. dentata and stachys can all work well. For a similar effect, you can also grow, without having to take them inside, salvias like *Salvia uliginosa* and *S.* 'Indigo Spires', as well as the more tender herbaceous varieties. There is *Vitex agnus-castus*, which is about 2 metres (6 feet) high, has a beautiful structure and comes in all shades of blue with fine silver leaves, and *Echium fastuosum*, as well as *Melianthus* which has very architectural silver leaves; I like the mixture of these blues with greys; and as groundcover, *Convolvulus sabatius* (syn. *C. mauritanicus*) with blue flowers.

Yellow is a particularly luminous colour, but if you are not careful it can be very bright, and I am very, very circumspect in how I use it. I once planted a *Phlomis fruticosa* between old-fashioned pink and burgundy roses and I had to cut all the flowers off every year because the yellow is so intense. I like yellows planted together – in a yellow border perhaps – and I like different tones of yellow together. I also like a laburnum walk because it is an isolated and big statement. I do not object to very pale yellows when they are carefully mixed. You can add a touch of yellow to a blue-mauve border, or you can use them with white. Most silver plants have yellow flowers and I tend to cut them off, but sometimes in a Mediterranean setting they can look just right. *Primula sikkimensis* is a very pretty yellow and I don't mind that colonizing my bog garden. Yellow is also good in a natural setting – with small narcissi and primroses. *Phlomis russeliana* with its tall yellow whorls is an architectural plant and looks very good with whites and green. Most early-flowering shrubs and herbaceous plants are yellow – there is a lot of yellow in the spring. Certainly in milder climates I try to plant *Ceanothus* and other blue plants for the early summer because

when you have finished with the daffodils and forsythia you have had enough of yellow.

Pale yellow works well with grey: I would like to plant a yellow and grey border – perhaps *Santolina punctata* subsp. *neapoletana* with *Achillea* 'Moonshine', *Rosa* 'Golden Wings' and *Clematis rehderiana* – which has pale yellow scented flowers – as well as the very pale yellow verbascums. For earlier in the season, *Paeonia mlokosewitschii* is good, and I also like *Phygelius aequalis* 'Yellow Trumpet' which is rather invasive but a wonderful pale yellow. Some shrubs, such as *Philadelphus coronarius* 'Aureus', *Sambucus racemosa* 'Sutherland Gold' and *S. r.* 'Plumosa Aurea', have attractive pale yellow leaves . There are some new hostas with good yellow variations and one of my favourite groundcover plants is *Euphorbia amygdaloides* var. *robbiae*, which is invasive but very effective in a woodland situation.

Oranges and russets are excellent colours for a later summer border. Somehow they reflect the mood in a garden at the end of the season. Orange mixes very well with dark-purple-leaved shrubs and herbaceous plants and grasses. *Euphorbia griffithii* 'Dixter' is early-flowering and has a dark leaves and bright orange flowers. Heleniums are useful, as is the purple-leaved fennel, *Foeniculum vulgare* 'Smokey', which also has tiny flat yellow flowers. There are some good orange dahlias like 'David Howard', orange ornamental poppies (forms of *Papaver orientale*) and pale orange *Fulva* 'Flore Pleno' are lovely, too. There are also now some handsome achilleas with orange flowers, like *Achillea* 'Terracotta' and *A.* 'Forncett Fletton'. Dark orange shades come from *Hemerocallis* 'Stafford', a deep brown-orange, and browny-claret *H.* 'Ed Murray'. Crocosmias are wonderful later in the summer, particularly 'Emily McKenzie',

'Lucifer' (which is the biggest) and 'Solfatare' (pale apricot with bronze-green leaves). I also love orange alstroemeria, which I like to mix with grasses and silvers.

I have always enjoyed white in the garden because it glows in the twilight, and is so calming and soothing. White works well in both city and country gardens, but needs to have an evergreen structure with it and silver plants to give it depth and soften it. White is a wonderful colour for framing the view of a wider landscape. When planted at the end of a garden, white flowers lengthen the view and give a feeling of distance as they allow the eye to travel on without restraint. For a white-flowered shrub I would choose *Cornus controversa* 'Variegata' or *C. alternifolia* 'Argentea' or indeed any other summer-flowering cornus. You can continue the white theme in herbaceous and mixed borders by underplanting with trilliums, a variety of small bulbs, scented smilacina, pulmonarias and variegated hostas. A plant I am never without is the white valerian because it seeds itself and its very pretty flowers go on and on – it doesn't seem to have a season. *Thalictrum delavayi* 'Album' and *T. tuberosum* are tall and airy and mix well with *Campanula latiloba* 'Alba', *Aster ericoides* 'Monte Cassino', *Verbascum chaixii* and *Selinum tenuifolium*.

year-round interest

Although almost everyone would agree that it is very pleasant to have something in flower throughout the year, many people put all their effort into the summer months. But it is particularly important to plant for the winter and early spring when there sometimes seems no hope of ever seeing a flower again. A plant like *Prunus* × *subhirtella* 'Autumnalis', which flowers all winter in milder areas, will give you hope for the future, as do the early-flowering hamamelis, *Lonicera* × *purpusii*, daphnes, the first hellebores and early cyclamen. Many early-flowering plants, like hamamelis, mahonia and *Viburnum farreri*, have the bonus of delicious fragrance. Of course, no garden should be without a little collection of snowdrops and at least one clump of *Iris unguicularis*.

Planting for autumn colour is important too – there are many wonderful trees and shrubs with leaves that change colour from early to late autumn, and thus extend the gardening season. A grove of *Acer japonicum* will range in colour from red to brown and yellow, and will be a fine sight all autumn. These bright colours mix very well with grasses as well as with shrubs with silver leaves. Good perennials for the autumn include the white *Aconitum* 'Ivorine' and the best blue aconitums, *A.* 'Spark's Variety' and *A. carmichaelii*; they are about 1 metre (3 feet) tall and are usually best in the back of the border. There are also the striking globe-headed agapanthus in different shades of blue and white and late-flowering Japanese anemones like the demure white *Anemone* 'Honorine Jobert' and the clear pink *A.* 'September Charm'. And there are all the asters: although I do not like the double *Aster novae-belgii*, for I think the flowers are coarse, I do like *A. amellus*, particularly 'King George' and 'Rosa Erfüllung', and I am very fond of *A.* 'Little Carlow', and all the forms of *A. ericoides*, *A. frikartii* and *A. lateriflorus*; these are all excellent in clouded drifts mixed with miscanthus and other grasses.

When I plant a border around a house, I always think of ways to keep it looking good all the year round. I position some architectural planting – yew hedges and box, perhaps – and then I add to the composition with slightly softer structural plants, such as clipped santolinas, skimmias or phlomis. I soften and link together this architectural structure with geraniums, salvias, thymes, alchemilla or stachys. I also plant clumps of either Hybrid Musk or Portland roses, which need little or no pruning and have the added bonus of being highly scented and of flowering right up to Christmas. If I need more upright shapes, I plant shrubs like rosemary 'Miss Jessopp's Upright' and *Berberis thunbergii* 'Dart's Red Lady'.

Above Spring colour is very important to me. At Gresgarth, *Prunus* 'Pink Shell' spreads its delicate haze of blossom over a small pond, with *Caltha palustris* var. *alba* at its edge, and the leaves of *Meconopsis nepalensis* and shoots of *Iris pseudacorus* 'Variegata' promise interest later in the year.

Right, above In the rose garden at Thorpe Hall, while *Rosa* 'Prosperity' brightens the beds in a summer display, the evergreen structure of tall Irish yews and cubes and edging of clipped box will look elegant throughout the year.

Right, below I planned the Madeira Walk borders at Ascott to look good well into autumn, with ornate pots planted with purple cordylines and repeated clumps of *Sedum* 'Herbstfreude' (Autumn Joy) and *Aster* × *frikartii* 'Mönch' providing glowing colour late in the year.

Pages 78–9 The purity and romance of a white garden, shining out against the rich greens of foliage and lawn. The tall spires of *Verbascum chaixii* 'Album' and the stems of *Lavandula angustifolia* 'Alba' push through the rounded forms and luscious blossoms of *Rosa* 'Iceberg'. On the arches, *R.* 'Sander's White Rambler' and 'Climbing Iceberg' promise more clouds of white to come.

Top The herb garden at La Bandiera, full of the scent of thyme, rosemary, lavender and chives, with fragrant orange trees in pots.
Above *Rhododendron luteum*, the most wonderfully perfumed of the azaleas, underplanted with *Tulipa* 'Helmar'.
Left The huge trumpets of *Cardiocrinum giganteum* var. *yunnanense* waft its powerful lily fragrance a considerable distance.

scent

One of the great pleasures of walking into the garden on a summer's evening is scent. It is a really important part of gardening – the aroma not only from flowers but also from the leaves and stems; it is such fun to rub a leaf for a wonderful smell. The earliest in the year is the pungent smell of hamamelis but sarcococca is also early and fragrant, and I always plant some under a window, or near a path, because it gives such a pleasure as you pass. *Populus lasiocarpa* and the balsam poplar *P. balsamifera* have sticky buds and a very sweet smell when the buds open in the early spring and should be planted in the lee of the prevailing wind so the scent is carried downwind. In late spring, there is the strong scent of *Rhododendron luteum*, the yellow species azalea, and all its hybrids. From then, all through the summer, I always have scented plants, whether those such as lavender, thyme or sage that release their scent only when touched, or others that have very scented flowers, like honeysuckle, viburnum, philadelphus – of which my favourites are *Philadelphus* 'Belle Etoile', 'Beauclerk' and 'Coupe d'Argent' – and *Azara*, a native of Chile, a shrub with evergreen leaves and small flowers that are very scented. I wouldn't be without *Skimmia laureola*, because the greenish-yellow flowers are very sweetly scented, and the leaves when crushed have an attractive pungent smell, nor *S. japonica* 'Fragrans', which has panicles of white flowers that smell of lily of the valley. And of course there is nothing like the scent of roses in high summer; the most scented of all is the damask rose, *Rosa* × *damascena*, which is used for attar of roses.

Other good scented plants include *Paeonia suffruticosa* 'Higurashi' and *P. rockii*, a branching shrub with large scented flowers that range in colour from white to deep burgundy; I have seen this in Italy, near Viterbo, where a peony-lover has planted a whole hillside of *rockii* seedlings – the scent is overwhelming. *Osmanthus* with its scented white flowers is a useful evergreen shrub, and *Mahonia japonica*, with ornamental evergreen pinnate leaves and terminal clusters of fragrant lemon-yellow flowers, is very scented. Tender scented shrubs include *Prostanthera*, a small greenhouse shrub from Australia which can be grown outside in milder climates – the leaves are very pungent; and *Laurelia sempervirens*, whose leaves are strongly aromatic when crushed. *Michelia*, a member of the magnolia family, has lovely scented flowers; it too is only suitable for milder areas.

Gardens in reliably warm areas, like the Mediterranean and California, have the best climates for releasing the scent of plants. In one garden, in southern Spain, I have planted orange and lemon trees, sweetly scented *Jasminum angulare* and *J. polyanthum* with rose-flushed white flowers, and *Lonicera hildebrandiana* – the giant honeysuckle with fragrant creamy-white flowers. There are daturas, crinum, *Osmanthus fragrans*, *Lilium formosanum*, which is 1 metre (3 feet) high and has white flowers with red or brown markings on the outside, and the wonderful *Heliotropium arborescens*, with its vanilla-scented flowers, which at Gresgarth I can only grow as an annual in pots. My heart lifts at the scent of *Viola* 'Coeur d'Alsace' or of *V. odorata*, which reminds me of my childhood – in the Mediterranean, as in much of Britain, it is often found growing in the wild. Also good are *Mirabilis jalapa*, a little corm that has bright yellow, pink or white flowers – not very pretty but strongly scented at night; and myrtle, with its fragrant flowers and leaves. In the heat, the leaves of lavender, sage, rosemary and the santolinas give out strong, dry aromas, redolent of the Mediterranean; even cypress has a wonderful scent if you touch the leaf.

In tropical gardens, scent is often only released at night – the daytime temperature is too high. In my experience the best tropical scented plants are *Cestrum nocturnum*, with its panicles of green flowers, and frangipani (*Plumeria*), which comes in different shades of pink, white and apricot; the scented flowers are little four-petalled cartwheels. Fragrant ylang-ylang (*Cananga odorata*), which should be in every tropical garden, has tiny green petals hanging in a twisted panicle.

practical aspects

All growing things, from trees to groundcover plants, should be chosen for their aesthetic qualities, both architectural and decorative; however, there are also practical considerations. Plants can be used to control soil erosion and fight atmospheric and sound pollution; they can also help to retain moisture. Where soil erosion through rain or wind is a problem, for example, the leaves and branches of trees and shrubs can act as deflecting canopies; trees or shrubs with multiple stems or branches can minimize the strength of the wind, while ground planting can also slow down water erosion. Fallen leaves increase the organic material in the soil, which in turn increases water absorption, and, under the ground, root systems hold the soil in place. Trees and shrubs can help control sound levels, by physically absorbing or diffusing sound, while the rustling of their leaves and stems can deflect attention from other noises.

All plants have an important role in combating atmospheric pollution through photosynthesis – the replacement of carbon dioxide in the air with oxygen. Plants can also play a part in temperature control, particularly in tropical and temperate climes; first by providing shade from the sun, but also by diffusing indirect light and heat. In a courtyard, for example, a wall planted with vines or other climbers will cut any heat reflected upwards from the paving.

At Little Malvern Court, hedges of box and yew and tall pleached hedges of lime shelter and screen the garden and frame the view.

Plants also act as temperature regulators by absorbing heat during the day, and slowly releasing it in the evening. I take all these practical issues into account when planning the planting of a garden.

shelter and screening

When what you want is a shelter belt or a screen from the traffic, you must plant evergreens because they are the most effective; they are also, *en masse*, rather dull, but a group becomes much more attractive if variegated, silver- or gold-leaved shrubs are mixed in. Large groupings of darker-leaved shrubs such as *Ilex aquifolium*, *Prunus lusitanica* or *Osmanthus heterophyllus* can be lightened by the addition of *Ligustrum ovalifolium* 'Argenteum' or *Ilex aquifolium* 'Silver Queen'; you could add to this silver-leaved shrubs such as *Olearia* × *scilloniensis* or *O. macrodonta*, sea buckthorn or *Cotoneaster franchetii*. These shrubs all work well and break up the monotony of the evergreens. *Griselinia littoralis*, with its fresh green leaves, also withstands the wind.

The same principle applies to trees. Suppose, for example, in a Mediterranean setting, you are planting a shelter belt of *Quercus ilex* and *Magnolia grandiflora*; even though the leaves of the two evergreens are contrasting, those of the holm oak small and dull, the magnolia's large and shiny, you would still want to break the monotony of the dark green with trees like *Cinnamomum camphora*, which has beautiful pale green young leaves. You might also want to break up the horizontal monotony by adding a group of vertical cypresses, planted in groups of three and five, and at a lower level, clumps of olive trees to bring in some silver, and maybe some deciduous flowering trees for interest through the seasons.

PLANTING SCHEMES

Different planting schemes can change the character of a garden dramatically. Plants can be used to make a statement, to be seen and noticed; they can also be used as a backdrop, or to frame and outline a view. To see how this works in practice, it is important for anybody interested in gardening to visit other people's gardens, to look and make an effort to see what is not immediately apparent. Inspiration may come simply from an interesting section of a herbaceous border, a group of shrubs or a well-planted pot. If you are considering incorporating any of the types of planting described below, it is especially useful to have seen, for instance, examples of herbaceous borders, wildflower meadows, woodland or topiary and hedges for yourself. By bringing to your own garden the planting ideas and combinations seen elsewhere, you can carry with you a feeling of the gardens that inspired you. You will, of course, never be able to imitate another garden completely, and nor should you want to – your garden is, and should remain, unique.

Designing borders and beds

Almost every border should have an architectural element within it to catch the eye and add structure. This can be provided in one of three ways: with herbaceous plants, where a particular plant is repeated at points along the border as a punctuation; by using clipped box or other similar regular-shaped plants, such as hebe or skimmia; or by interposing pots or urns into the overall design of the bed. Any architectural feature used should of course be in proportion to the height and length of the planting. All of these elements act as visual devices which divide the border and relieve the eye, while still maintaining the planting flow. In a large garden, architecture like this will help to break up or frame plants, which might otherwise look very flimsy on their own.

When planning the outline of a border, you don't need to equate straight lines with formal design, nor curved lines with informality: the formality or informality comes from the planting design. I tend to prefer straight edges; they are simpler and often more successful, and they can always be softened by plants spilling over them. Beds and borders that are bounded by straight lines are easier to design and execute in the garden than those with complicated flowing lines. They are practical and economical: straight edges are easier to maintain and there is a bonus in that any edging paving does not have to be cut into difficult shapes.

Of course, in some cases curves are necessary; for example borders in an informal part of the garden may have to curve to follow a path or the edge of a pond. In a woodland garden where the borders follow the contours of the land, you will curve the borders to follow those contours. Even in a formal setting I sometimes think that curved borders might add to the character and charm of the garden, but in these situations I tend to design the curves with a regular rhythm. Curves should be used with controlled restraint or they will look fussy and contrived.

Sometimes the constraints of the plot seem to demand curves. I have designed in Edinburgh a garden which is very long and narrow, and the land slopes quite dramatically downwards. By curving the borders on both sides in a regular pattern I am giving myself wider scope for an interesting planting design as well as a strong rhythm all the way down the garden. There are also occasions where curves are an intrinsic part of the layout and the whole design of the garden and landscape flows around them. In one of my projects I designed two circular gardens enclosed by yew hedges with a curved path, hedge and trees which linked the gardens to form a very organic pattern of grass, hedges and trees.

A circular border is particularly complicated to plant for it is difficult to give it a consistent rhythm. However, this can be done by repeating a plant at intervals round the circle, or by planting a continuous ribbon all the way round. The centre is best planted with one variety of plant, either in a cruciform shape or in graduated circles, like a dartboard. With such a border I like to be very regular in the planting. An irregular or serpentine border also needs a rhythm in the planting. If you accentuate the convex points of a border with repeat planting this will foreshorten the view, and introduce a dramatic rhythm. If, on the other hand, the repeat planting is on the inside of the curve, the effect will be more natural and the rhythm more informal. In smaller borders and in town gardens, the rhythm and textural differences must also be reduced to scale.

Clockwise from top left At Ascott, clumps of *Hosta sieboldiana* alternating with clumps of *Skimmia* x *confusa* 'Kew Green' impressively line a long border that links one garden with another. At Las Navas, I placed terracotta pots filled with white petunias at regular intervals to add interest in a narrow border planted with 'Iceberg' roses and *Iris* 'New Snow'. A woodland border with repeated plantings of white azaleas (*Rhododendron* 'Palestrina'). A border edged with a line of *Hosta plantaginea* var. *japonica* in front of *Philadelphus* 'Manteau d'Hermine'. Another simple but graphic planting, below the wisteria tunnel at Château le Belvedere, of *Nepeta* 'Six Hills Giant' above *Geranium ibericum*.

shrub borders

Shrub borders should be large enough for each chosen plant to grow to its full size. If shrubs have to be cut back they will usually lose their natural shape; what is more, it adds to the work. Of course, sometimes I need a particular shrub in a border because its shape, scent or colour is necessary for the success of the design, even if this will entail its being pruned, and some shrubs still look good after clipping. I don't mass the shrubs at the very edge of the border; I like leaving plenty of space for a variety of groundcover plants, which make the maintenance easier and add to the interest of the planting. This area of low plants can vary from 50 centimetres (1 1/2 feet) to 2 metres (6 feet), with the taller shrubs rising through the groundcover; this gives the border some breathing space and is visually more pleasant than being faced with a barrage of tall plants to the front of the border.

In an informal border, you should position shrubs in a staggered, almost random way, always trying to imagine how these shrubs would look in nature with the groundcover spreading underneath them in natural drifts and swathes. This means always avoiding straight lines and sometimes, perhaps, placing a taller shrub near the front.

On the whole I prefer not to include herbaceous planting in shrub borders, apart from groundcover plants, because it makes the border look spotty and the individual herbaceous plants look out of place. There are exceptions, of course: I would allow the inclusion of very large sweeps of foxgloves, *Epilobium angustifolium* var. *album*, meadowsweet, *Iris sibirica* or *I. ensata*, geraniums, Japanese anemones and some of the taller grasses, because these big drifts will seem natural.

In general, when I have to plan a large border I start with a background of evergreen shrubs like *Viburnum tinus*, choisya and osmanthus, together with silver-leaved or variegated shrubs like *Rhamnus alaternus*; in a mild climate I might try *Pittosporum tenuifolium* 'Silver Queen'. For silver-leaved shrubs I like using *Elaeagnus umbellata,* which also happens to have very scented, tiny white flowers, and *E. angustifolia*, which is even more silver, with willow-like leaves and scented white flowers.

When height and silver is needed I usually plant *Pyrus salicifolia* 'Pendula', which if necessary can be kept to the desired size and shape by clipping in spring. With these basic architectural plants I have clumps of large shrub roses like *Rosa rugosa* or Hybrid Musks or any of the species roses which also have berries – mixing them with deciduous shrubs like philadelphus and deutzia. In front of those I would plant smaller roses and silver-leaved plants. I very much like shrubs with burgundy-coloured leaves and I often plant *Cotinus coggygria* 'Royal Purple', which I clip to the size I need, always trying to keep the shape as natural as possible. Other effective burgundy-leaved plants include *Pittosporum tenuifolium* 'Purpureum' and *P. t.* 'Nigricans', as well as *Berberis thunbergii* 'Dart's Red Lady' and *B. t.* 'Bagatelle'.

When I combine plants I usually mix these dark-leaved shrubs with yellow and buff or pink flowers. If on the other hand I wanted a completely yellow border then I would use shrubs like *Philadelphus coronarius* 'Aureus', or *Aralia elata* 'Aureovariegata'. I would add yellow- or white-flowered shrubs and some groundcover such as *Lupinus arboreus* 'Golden Spire' or *L. a.* 'Snow Queen' – and *Phlomis fruticosa* or *P. russeliana* if you need more of an accent plant, adding perhaps a touch of blue.

herbaceous borders

A herbaceous border is really a collection of plants – for lovers of plants, it is a way of satisfying their appetite for them. But it is also like painting a picture, because in a defined space you can concentrate a lot of colour and shapes. As the plants die down, it need have no permanent structure.

When I started designing gardens – about twenty years ago – herbaceous borders were out of fashion; they were considered expensive and time-consuming and people couldn't be bothered to maintain them. Instead, they wanted mixed borders and old-fashioned rose gardens. Now, herbaceous borders are fashionable again: perhaps because so much has been written about them; perhaps because people are spending more time in and more money on their gardens; and perhaps because there are so many thousands of wonderful plants available.

To my mind there are two sorts of herbaceous planting. The traditional border, much influenced by Gertrude Jekyll, is colour-themed and, ideally, in flower continuously from spring until autumn. This sort of planting particularly suits more traditional architecture and design, in situations like that at Eaton Hall, where the borders are wide and very long and are situated beneath tall retaining walls. When I started working at Eaton, the borders were mainly planted with shrubs and a few herbaceous plants and looked very uninspiring. I felt that the terraces were so grand, architecturally, that they needed to be balanced by strong, simple ideas, so I planted themed, predominantly single-colour herbaceous borders throughout the garden.

The layout of a traditional herbaceous border is structured, not with architectural divisions but with plants: tall plants at the back and lower ones at the front. At the back are plants like delphiniums, tall campanulas, inula, scaling down to plants of medium size –

Campanula latifolia, phlox, eryngiums, then to nepeta and geraniums and, at ground level, helianthemums and dianthus.

When I plant very long herbaceous borders, I like to structure and break the length with architectural features such as pots, or blocks of yew or box. In some cases I may repeat a particular plant at regular intervals all the way down the border. A good example of this was the Madeira Walk at Ascott House – a very long and narrow herbaceous border running along a high wall; I not only broke it up but repeated some of the plants in order to lead the eye the length of the border. To give a more homogenous air to a border I do like to repeat the same groups of plants all the way along. I also like to mix grasses of different heights, through which you can see other herbaceous plants like poppies, verbascum and echinacea.

I sometimes put tall plants in the front of the border – that is to say I plant them in a more natural manner than in the traditional border; I might plant a clump of delphiniums in the centre of the bed instead of conventionally at the back, with perhaps achillea and verbascum threading their way through other plants. There should never be gaps at the front of the border; any spaces should be filled either with low-growing herbaceous plants or, to alter the balance and proportions of the design, the occasional tall plant.

Below, left to right *Cornus controversa* spreads its branches over *Matteuccia struthiopteris* and the flowers of *Rhododendron* 'Sylphides' and *R. augustinii* 'Werrington' and white and pink candelabra primulas, with the small *Betula utilis* var. *jacquemontii* 'Grayswood Ghost' to one side. A woodland border at Eaton Hall, with *Elaeagnus angustifolia*, Spanish bluebells, and white colour from *Cornus florida* and *Rhododendron* 'Dora Amateis'. The blue-mauve herbaceous border at Gresgarth, with *Geranium* 'Johnson's Blue', *Euphorbia dulcis* 'Chameleon' and *Papaver orientale* 'Patty's Plum'. The mixed colours of 'Indian Chief' irises, orange poppies, white *Verbascum chaixii* 'Album' and *V.* 'Cotswold Queen'.

Even though I admire colourful herbaceous borders, I prefer to work through the range of a single colour. That doesn't mean that I only want, say, blues and whites in a blue border. Sometimes a touch of red or burgundy in a blue border, or orange in a pink border, can make an impressive contrast.

The other sort of herbaceous planting, currently very fashionable, is much more naturalistic. Grasses and perennial plants like achillea, echinacea, verbascum, helenium, salvia, *Lychnis coronaria*, filipendula, poppies, alliums, geraniums and day lilies are used together to emulate the natural growth that you might find in the wild. The emphasis is on grouping plants that would grow together in their natural habitat – plants for meadows, plants for moist shade and so on – so that you do not have one plant taking over from another: you mix plants that all like being in that particular habitat to the same degree.

This naturalistic planting differs from the traditional border in that there are broader expanses of planting and bigger drifts of the same plant; there are many more grasses, and the whole effect is softer and much less structured. Plantings in this style do not work on a small scale – the scheme must be a big gesture with huge drifts of plants over large areas.

The best examples of this new border planting style can be seen in Germany, Holland and in the United States, particularly in the work of Wolfgang Oehme and James van Sweden. These more naturalistic borders work well in America and continental Europe and also in the hotter, drier counties of England: a particularly attractive aspect is that the plants used often take on wonderful colours in autumn, and have flower heads that look good throughout the winter. However, as many of these plants naturally like a drier, well-drained environment, in wetter areas naturalistic borders can look sodden and moth-eaten, especially by the end of the summer.

Herbaceous borders should always be planted in a clearly defined area: I don't like them isolated in the centre of the lawn where there is no background or design structure. Planting like this needs a visual backdrop such as a shrub border or a hedge. A herbaceous border in a lawn has to be big enough to be the main feature, as at Bramdean House in Hampshire where the two herbaceous borders are some of the best I know, commanding as they do most of the view from the house.

Right, top to bottom Among *Penstemon* 'Hewitt's Pink', *Rosa* 'Mevrouw Nathalie Nypels' and *Sisyrinchium striatum*, repeated plantings of box cubes and lavender 'Loddon Pink' give structure to this long pink border at Ascott. A view of my Chelsea 1995 garden, showing how effective small sections of red are in a predominantly white border. The hot border at Eaton Hall glows with *Monarda* 'Cambridge Scarlet', *Macleaya* 'Kelway's Coral Plume' and *Digitalis ferruginea*.

Left A predominantly white planting with *Allium nigrum* and *Philadelphus coronarius* set off by dark *Delphinium* 'Faust' and little mauve *Viola cornuta*.

Right Deep reds, purples and blues from *Iris* 'Indian Chief', *Allium hollandicum* 'Purple Sensation' and *Anchusa azurea* 'Loddon Royalist'.

Below A closer view of a red section of border in my Chelsea garden for 1995. *Convolvulus cneorum* adds a touch of silver between red *Dahlia* 'Bednall Beauty' and a grouping of *Iris* 'Kent Pride', *Cytisus* 'Boskoop' and *Heuchera micrantha* var. *diversifolia* 'Palace Purple'.

Clockwise from top left Two views of the colourful rhododendron planting under the trees at Gresgarth. A carpet of bluebells by the ruined tower in the woods at Gresgarth, enlivened by a touch of bright red flower colour from *R.hododendron* 'Elizabeth'. The wonderfully decorative *Exochorda* x *macrantha* 'The Bride' with *Tulipa* 'White Triumphator' and dark hellebores in the woodland walk at Eaton Hall. A woodland planting of *Bergenia* 'Silberlicht' and dicentra.

woodland gardens

If you have an area of existing woodland you will usually need to open it up in order to create new planting spaces, so clearance is the first task. The canopy of the trees should be high enough to give some shade, but also allow plenty of light and air for your later planting, so you should always start by taking out the least important, fast-growing species – which might be trees like birch or hazel – leaving important, slow-growing trees, such as oak, beech and ash. In fact, I believe that you should always leave an oak in preference to everything else, including beech, but that is a question of personal taste, and beech does have a wonderful shape, as well as autumn colour.

It is important to choose the right trees for the climate and, where possible, to use trees that are indigenous to the area. Each area of America, for example, has a different indigenous oak, *Quercus velutina* coming from the east and central parts, *Q. virginiana* from the south-east of the United States and Mexico and *Q. rubra* (the red oak), from east and north America. Although some can be planted in different areas, others will not grow as well outside their normal habitat; *Q. phellos*, for instance, though native to the east of the States, can be used in the south, but *Q. lobata* (the valley oak), which comes from California, cannot be grown on the East Coast.

After choosing which trees will form the basis of the woodland, the next thing to do is to make the paths; a woodland path should never be straight, but always curved, following other natural, existing contours. There should be contrast in a woodland garden, and one area should lead into another – a narrow, heavily planted path could lead into an open, sunny glade, for example; I like the sensation of open and closed spaces as well as the look of sunlit areas that contrast with areas where there is a heavier canopy.

A mistake that is sometimes made, and which I myself made in my own woodland in Lancashire, is to be over-enthusiastic about the planting of shrubs. One tends to forget how large shrubs can become and it is very important that they should be planted in a natural manner, leaving them to grow in a way that allows gaps and spaces in the woodland. It is also important to have a mixture of evergreen and deciduous shrubs – particularly in the winter when the evergreen planting should

be solid and act as a framework for the deciduous shrubs.

Woodland gardens are particularly good in extreme climates, where they will be the main source of planting pleasure throughout the year. For example, in a garden I am designing in Canada, south of Montreal, the climate is so severe that, apart from a very small area around the house, the land is given over to the most beautiful wood of white oak and sugar, red and silver maples, which is carpeted with trilliums and ferns. If the natural groundcover in a woodland is attractive, there is no particular need to plant much additional cover. It depends on what kind of woodland garden you prefer: the natural one where you plant trees, shrubs and a few bulbs and wait to see what else emerges through the undergrowth; or the planned one where you create large borders filled with appropriate plants such as epimediums, cyclamen, hellebores, primroses and ferns. In such a border, plants should be grown in large drifts, and there should also be some shrubs – perhaps some of the smaller rhododendrons and azaleas, skimmia for its marvellous scent, and enkianthus and various ferns, all of which will make the area look as natural as possible. If

however the area is small, you can indulge in more compact groups of all sorts of small groundcover plants. It is important to have both colour and scent in a woodland garden – a group of hamamelis will really brighten and perfume a winter's day and *Daphne bholua* gives out its wonderful scent from midwinter to the middle of spring.

If you have to start your woodland garden from scratch, it is obviously important to carry out a soil analysis of the site to see what the conditions are, so that you can plant accordingly. You then outline the overall design: paths, clumps, rides, and so on. You choose which will be the dominant species through the plantation – for instance, oak, beech, horse chestnut – and mix these with some quick-growing 'nurse' trees: these could be Scots pine or ash or, in wet areas, birch, bird cherry (*Prunus padus*) or alder. If you want an immediate effect you could plant a few large trees; this would give immediate shade and height. The distances between the trees when fully grown must be calculated, and the young trees planted at those distances. Evergreen shrubs such as hollies, *Viburnum tinus*, *Prunus laurocerasus* and cotoneasters will provide shelter and an instant framework.

wildflower meadows

Wildflower meadows, though utterly charming, are an illusion – there is nothing wild or artless about them. Difficult and slow to achieve (a proper wildflower meadow can take twenty-five years to establish), they are contrived, expensive and labour-intensive. Although their popularity in our ecologically aware times has increased and many people are interested in the idea of having a wildflower garden, they are not easy to establish. The reason is that wildflowers can easily be taken over by the coarser grasses and in order to eliminate these thugs you must weaken the fertility of the soil. You also have to take care what you plant – you cannot grow wildflowers that do not naturally flourish in the local soil; or, if you do, you will have to replant them every year.

There are many caveats, the most important being that you must choose your location carefully. If you have newly planted trees and shrubberies in the same area the annual feed given to the trees will encourage tougher grasses to grow, thus stifling the wildflowers. Equally, in order to discourage tough grasses from taking over, you should mow when the first flush of flowers has faded, in spring, then again in late summer, and then give a last cut before the winter, taking away the cuttings each time. This means that you cannot plant bulbs in that area.

Having said that, I have designed several meadows and it can be worth the effort to make them, because they look so pretty if you succeed. The nice thing is that you do not need a large garden to have a wildflower meadow – you can have one, for example, instead of a lawn. I personally dislike large areas of lawn which have to be mown regularly, and would much rather see wide paths cut through long grass.

The soil should be analysed, and a survey taken of any existing flora on the proposed site and in the surrounding area to see what species are indigenous. The poorer the soil the better it is for a wildflower meadow; if the soil is too rich then

Left, top to bottom Topiary domes of golden yew peep over a clipped yew hedge that edges a wildflower meadow at Eaton Hall. Wildflowers and long grass, with willows and plumed miscanthus in the watermeadows at Stanbridge Mill. In this London garden, strips are rotavated and seed sown every year so that cornfield annuals like poppies, cornflowers and corncockles can grow.
Right The annual flowers of the old cornfields are also grown in yearly rotavated and seeded ground at Ascott House, within formal patterns and mown grass paths. Apple trees, *Prunus avium* and *Quercus ilex* rise above the sea of flowers and long grass, while buttresses of yew create separate enclosures for the meadow planting.

it may be worth removing the topsoil (reusing it elsewhere) and rotavating sand into the remaining subsoil. It is important that there is no vegetation left at all, particularly hidden weed seeds. Then, preferably in spring, an appropriate wildflower mix should be sown, and rolled in.

Even though my advice on how to make a wildflower meadow derives from many years of trial and error, I still come across unforeseen difficulties: in one garden, for example, the whole wildflower area was suddenly invaded by thistles. We either had to use weedkiller over the whole area and start again, or kill the weeds in selected areas, or individually dead-head and pull out each thistle. We decided to spot-treat individual plants with weedkiller, and then mow the infested areas at regular intervals over the year to reduce the thistles' vigour.

Most people think that a wildflower meadow will flower as abundantly every year as the first, or that it will be constantly blooming with poppies, cornflowers and corncockles. However, these more showy plants are annuals which appear in newly dug ground, and traditionally colonize fields which are ploughed regularly. If that is what you want you will have to imitate that process by rotavating the ground annually just as you would in a cornfield. I often suggest that strips in a wildflower area are rotavated, sometimes with a pattern, and the areas sown with annual seeds.

vegetable and herb gardens

In the last few years vegetable gardens have become fashionable. This is partly because they appeal to the many people who want to grow their own wholesome food, and partly because of the renewed popularity of the potager, or ornamental vegetable garden, where the garden is laid out as decoratively as possible, with beds in formal or geometric patterns filled with vegetables planted together with ornamental flowers. Probably the greatest of all ornamental vegetable gardens is the one at Villandry, near Tours in France. There the huge parterre of box is divided into nine large squares with vegetables planted in geometrically fashioned beds. The most influential modern example is Rosemary Verey's small potager at Barnsley House in Gloucestershire. Its attraction comes partly from contemplating the standard roses, enticing arbours, neatly patterned box beds and pretty but practical brick paths, and partly in knowing that the rows of salads, vegetables and fruit they contain will be delicious to eat.

When I was a child in Italy we had a large, very functional kitchen garden and I remember well the taste of our own fresh fruit and vegetables, which were beyond comparison. I am always happy therefore when asked to design one for a client. However, although I have designed many ornamental vegetable gardens, I prefer to make them where there is a real wish to use the garden as a practical, functioning space and not merely as an ornament to be admired, since growing vegetables is a most laborious form of gardening, particularly when you employ – as you should – safer but time-consuming organic methods of cultivation.

I have always admired the way that the French prune and train their fruit trees and wherever possible I try to introduce such imaginative features as apple trees trained as step-overs, goblets or espaliers, fan-trained or cordoned. In any parts of the plot which are not planted with vegetables I either establish grassy areas with fruit trees, or design borders for cut flowers. In a smaller vegetable garden I will still design a pattern of beds, but plant them with proportionately more vegetables and fewer flowers.

I am also happy to design herb gardens, but I consider culinary herbs a practical feature, and even though I admire wonderful set pieces such as the herb garden at Sissinghurst, I think the most important thing about a herb garden is that it should be planted near the kitchen so that the herbs can be easily used. To plant a herb garden that looks attractive can be difficult, because the plants are often of lax habit and tend to flop, as well as being very troublesome to maintain. So when I make a herb garden I rely on repetitions of plants like *Iris* 'Florentina', thyme, hyssop and chives to give a varied texture and some structure to the garden.

Opposite, left In the new beds I created in the kitchen garden at Ascott House, the vegetables and salad plants are grown in neat rows and arranged so that their different colours make a pleasing pattern. The beds are then edged with apples trained as step-overs. Other beds are edged with clipped box in geometric patterns.

Opposite, right For the herb garden at La Bandiera I designed an intricate geometric layout of small beds separated by paving in pretty patterns of square brick and pebbles. Lemon and orange trees grow in decorative terracotta pots, surrounded by herbs such as chives, thyme and rosemary, and fragrant shrubs like santolina.

Below left An avenue of bamboo poles frames a view over the vegetable garden at Gresgarth, back to the house. As well as vegetables and herbs I grow flowers for cutting, and these 2.5 metres (8 feet) poles support sweet peas.

Below In the herb garden at Château le Belvedere, hyssop and golden marjoram surround an ornamental stone basin.

Opposite, above In the herb garden at Château le Belvedere, an ornate wooden seat is backed by a yew hedge. Buttresses project from the hedge, and neat clipped box balls on either side of the seat contrast with the softer, informal shapes of the herbs, including hyssop, artemisia, purple sage, golden marjoram and tree onion.

Left, above Clipped box edged with rope tiles makes a neat surround for large beds containing vegetables, flowers and fruit in the walled kitchen garden at Gresgarth. Within the beds, bamboo frames surround pear trees being trained into goblet shapes. Marigolds provide companion planting for carrots.

Opposite, below In the kitchen garden at Château le Belvedere, large formal beds are elegantly edged with box clipped at the corners into spheres. They contain both vegetables and decorative climbing plants like honeysuckle, roses and sweet peas trained on supports. In the central octagon, a patterned lead fountain is surrounded by a pretty, tapestry-like arrangement of thymes with different foliage colours interwoven and cushions of 'Hidcote' lavender. In the four corners of the square surrounding the fountain are simple bench seats shaded by trelliswork arbours inspired by those at Villandry.

Left, below In the kitchen garden at Gresgarth, beautifully turned finials painted a glossy dark burgundy top the posts that support the wires for espaliered apples. Vegetables are planted amid a jumble of flowers including nasturtiums, roses and sweet peas.

Left At Eaton Hall, I restored the Victorian parterre in the Dragon Fountain Garden, returning the patterns of the beds, which had been altered into severe geometric lines, to their original, more graceful curved shapes. However, I did not attempt to imitate a typical Victorian planting of a mixture of bright-coloured bedding plants and multi-coloured gravel. Instead I chose a red theme, realized in plants whose colours range from dark burgundy to pale pink. In spring the beds are filled with bright red and maroon tulips with dark red and orange wallflowers. *Bergenia* 'Silberlicht' surrounds the planted bowl on a pedestal.

knots, parterres and mazes

Knots, parterres and mazes are patterns made from plants, usually hedging plants of various sizes. A knot is an elaborate interwoven pattern made from low hedging material such as box, in a configuration that can vary from elaborate interlacing to complex or simple geometrical patterns; knot gardens are designed to be viewed from above or from a window. Knot gardens can also be made of thyme, rosemary, teucrium or santolina; in a vegetable or herb garden, chives or parsley can also be used. They were particularly popular in Tudor England, and today are a happy addition to a formal garden – a way of dealing with an empty space which is mainly viewed from above. I am at the moment designing a garden in Ireland, with a shady courtyard area which needs to look attractive and inviting so I have designed it as a knot garden with a fountain in the centre.

A knot garden makes an excellent feature for a small town garden, but in a larger garden, a parterre would be more appropriate; this was the traditional way of dealing with a large, flat area. A parterre is an arrangement of elaborate and symmetrically patterned beds. Designed on a far larger scale than a knot garden, the hedging is traditionally box, but in the nineteenth century the patterns began to be cut out of grass, or made in gravel. Roses and other shrubs, particularly low-growing ones, can also be used as edging; in the past they were often combined with coloured gravel to make patterns. When, at Eaton Hall, I restored one of the parterres originally designed in the nineteenth century by William Nesfield, although I reproduced the original pattern, I did not try to be faithful to the original infilling of bedding plants and coloured gravel that Nesfield would probably have used, since the gaudy colours employed, historically, in the planting schemes in parterres were not always very attractive.

Sometimes in a garden, a maze can be an interesting alternative to a parterre. A maze can be strictly geometric or of more random design, formal or informal – usually depending on the plants chosen: any maze with a clipped box hedge could be defined as formal, but a maze using bamboo perhaps, or lavender would be intrinsically informal. The informal maze at Glendurgan, in Cornwall, is of cherry laurel (*Prunus laurocerasus*) clipped in asymmetrical shape, on a slope and with narrow paths. It is viewed from above and its irregular design means that the romantic aspect of the site remains intact.

Centre, far left In the library garden at Ascott I made a knot with clipped hedges and domes of box, which I infilled with lavender. The intricate crisscrossing lines of the knot contrast with the great solid blocks of yew that edge this part of the garden.

Centre, left Another view of the Dragon Fountain Garden at Eaton Hall, showing how effective are the patterns of a parterre when filled with a restrained colour palette and neutral gravel. The clipped domes and cones of yew and box are important, too, for giving structure, punctuation and definition to the garden.

Bottom, far left On either side of the top terrace at Eaton Hall (which is divided by two double rows of pleached limes) I designed a graceful modern parterre whose quatrefoil plats are simply cut out of the grass and infilled with plain gravel. The terrace, though high, is looked down on from the house, which is why I chose a parterre – a ground pattern – to fill it. The bold, graphic design suits the wide space and elevated position of the terrace.

Bottom, middle This modern parterre at Cock Crow Farm consists of solid geometric patterns of box. Some beds are simple flat box platforms; in some, the box rises into sharp-edged pyramids; in others, pots planted with santolina are inserted so that the contrasting silver-blue foliage emerges in domes from the blocks of green.

Left A parterre or knot is a good design to fill a large courtyard, and so in the new entrance courtyard at La Bandiera – formed by the building of two new wings at right angles to the main house – I gave the fountain pool an edging of box and surrounded it with a pattern of broad, flat rectangles of box and lavender, with clipped cones emerging from the box. This planting was also practical: the courtyard is the roof of an underground garage, so the soil is very shallow and dry – conditions that box and lavender do not mind.

Topiary, the art of shaping trees and shrubs into recognisable form, has been admired and practised since Roman times, revived in the Renaissance and much used in England and France during the seventeenth century. Box and yew are the shrubs most often used, but you can also train foliage climbers, such as small-leaved ivy, to cover a metal topiary frame. Topiary is a flight of imagination, an amusement and should be used with discretion. Although I do not use much topiary, preferring to clip and shape lightly, there are situations when it is fun to shape a hedge in a certain way. I usually prefer to do so using controlled, geometric shapes, like blocks and ziggurats, rather than cut-outs of animals and people.

Topiary can be used as a centrepiece, a type of sculpture or ornament, and can be modern or traditional. You can use it effectively in a small garden as a simple focal point or as an architectural feature: designs might include tall pyramids of ivy in pots, or shiny-leaved Portugal laurels clipped into standard trees. *Viburnum tinus*, lavender and rosemary can be clipped and trained – in fact there are many plants that can be used as topiary. Trees like crataegus, *Sorbus aria,* or *Pyrus salicifolia* 'Pendula' can also be trained into shapes, and I often use the last to add height in a pale border. I have even seen rosemary trained as an espalier against a wall, and on the side of a dovecote door at Bramdean House. Holly will form a wonderful, huge mound as well as making smaller shapes.

F,or me, nothing compares with yew because it clips best of all, and the dark green of its leaves is denser and richer than any other. However, I was greatly inspired by the gardens at Drummond Castle where I saw for the first time some very large *Prunus cerasifera* 'Nigra', which had been clipped as round standards and used as central features in the enormous parterre. I had always thought of this tree as rather dusty – dark and vulgar – but the way it had been clipped at Drummond meant that the red leaves looked fresh and took on

a pink translucent glow against the sun. Since then I have used this tree often: both in my own garden and at Ascott House where it is planted all the way along the long terrace, acting as an architectural link, as well as bringing colour into the border at a high level without casting shade.

Where the climate is more extreme, architectural evergreen shapes are important for year-round structure and decorative effect, but topiary plants must be able to withstand the more severe conditions. In America, for example, on the East Coast, privet is best for hedges and topiary, while in Texas, *Ilex cornuta*, *I. opaca* and *Magnolia grandiflora* 'Claudia Wannamaker' are more popular.

Right, top to bottom A small triangular maze of box. Clipped blocks and spheres of box provide perfect punctuation points at the end of paths and borders. The designs for topiary shapes for the astrological garden at Ascott House. The decorative shape of a spiral emerging from a little square of box. A neat, dome-shaped cushion of box, a simple shape to clip, and effective in the smallest of spaces.
Below A very elegant use of topiary in the gardens of Château le Belvedere. A grand yew hedge has been clipped with ruler-like precision and sculpted into an arched doorway with an elaborate pediment and gracefully curving 'walls'. In the centre is a spiral of box, and, behind a massive buttress, a fastigiate hornbeam has been clipped into an even more immaculately tidy shape.

Below left The art of clipping plants into deliberate shapes is suitable for the smallest gardens as well as large, grand ones. This parterre in a small city garden uses a variety of geometric shapes for ornamental effect, and combines flashes of golden box to embellish the pattern made by the more common *Buxus sempervirens*. Portugal laurel clipped as standards add height and further decoration.

Right One of the four expertly clipped pedimented yew archways that lead to four separate gardens at Château le Belvedere. Monumental and impressive now, the yew was planted at 30 centimetres (12 inches) high, and had reached the desired height in only ten years. I always prefer to plant hedging as small, young plants that can get used to the soil and be clipped as they grow.

Far right At Château le Belvedere we collected all the topiary box shapes that were scattered around the park and brought them together to make the centrepiece for the garden. Surrounded by low, neat box hedges, the impact of the elaborately sculpted shapes is vastly increased by their being positioned together.

Below right At Gresgarth I rescued a golden yew that had fallen in a storm but not died; I had a metal frame in the shape of a lion made, and placed it so that the yew could grow through it and be clipped round it.

Below middle right I often use topiary at the entrance to a house where its bold simplicity can be highly effective, introducing the house without competing with it. For the entrance courtyard at Thorpe Hall I designed a topiary parterre with blocks of box interspersed with tall pyramids of yew and enclosed with lines of box decorated with little domes.

Below far right Topiary can be a chance to add charming individual touches to an overall garden design, as the gardeners at Ascott House did when they carved out this elephant to decorate a hedging arch.

A FORMAL GARDEN

Château le Belvedere

Château le Belvedere, the home of the King and Queen of the Belgians, lies on the outskirts of Brussels, surrounded by a park. A Neo-Palladian mansion, it was built in the late eighteenth century and presented to King Leopold II in the nineteenth century. A few years after Queen Paola, then the Princess of Liège, went to live there in the late 1970s, she asked me to help her with the garden. It was my first large project.

Le Belvedere is built on high ground, and its park and gardens fall away from the house towards a distant view of the city of Brussels. In the nineteenth century, a formal garden had been built below the house with a large number of very wide steps leading down to it. It consisted of a vast terrace with small formal beds edged in box and planted with Hybrid Tea roses of all colours. Looking down on to it from the windows of the château, I was struck by how grim this parterre looked, particularly when seen in relation to the landscape beyond; and when walking on the terrace I felt no sense of space or belonging. This rigid, sparse design did not suit the Queen, who had a keen interest in plants and colour combinations and

a penchant for English gardens such as Sissinghurst and Hidcote, which she visited regularly. She wanted a more intimate garden in which she could indulge her love of plants: a garden with a profusion of flowers and scent. At the same time, the garden had to look interesting all year round when seen from the house above. Thus it needed a clearly defined structure that would provide a satisfying pattern.

The idea of designing a garden in the form of a Persian carpet took shape. The pattern of the 'carpet' would be made up of yew and box hedges combined with trees, and many different flowering plants would give it colour. Tall, thick yew hedges would be used to define the planted areas. Each was to have a different character. Some would have brick paths laid in different geometric patterns. To frame the carpet I designed a metal pergola which runs the length of it on one side and is planted with *Wisteria floribunda* 'Alba'; on the other I planted a walk of pleached lime trees, underplanted with spring-flowering bulbs. Lime allées are traditional in Belgium, as are yew hedges. Both contribute to the contrast I wanted to achieve

between evergreen and deciduous trees. The yew and box patterns also provide something to look at all year round, especially in winter. Deciduous trees such as the limes and cherries change as the garden's colour unfolds through the year.

When we first planted the yew hedges they were only 30 centimetres (1 foot) high; I prefer to plant small shrubs that get used to the soil and that can be clipped as they grow. A problem with the trend these days for instant gardens is that when you plant larger shrubs, which are used to growing in a different soil and a different climate, they often fail to thrive and have to be replaced. In this case the yews grew very fast, and after only six years they were already over 1 metre (3 feet) tall.

You reach the gardens from a long flight of steps, which lead down from a gravelled walk below the château. From above you see a parterre, but as you approach the bottom of the steps the designs become more complicated, and you are enticed to enter the hedged area. The design satisfies all requirements. Seen from above, the area has a formal, geometric grandeur with a pattern and a central motif, but as you walk into the design, the impression changes and you find yourself in a garden with several enclosures, each intimate and private. Once you are inside, the spaces enfold you and you are no longer aware of the house or anything else outside.

At the centre of the carpet, there is a large octagon of grass. Topiary shapes of box moved from other areas in the park provide a centrepiece for the octagon. The central topiary is tall and the box hedges are low. They are interplanted with 'Lavender Lassie' roses and the wild annual meadow flowers (corncockles, cornflowers, poppies) which the Queen loves. From the octagon, four small wooden gates surrounded by a beautifully clipped pedimented yew archway lead to the four separate gardens: an early summer garden, a yellow garden, an old-fashioned rose garden and a small herb and fruit garden.

As you enter the early summer garden, there are two standard *Viburnum carlesii* on either side, but your eye is caught by the main feature: a cruciform brick pattern surrounding four square beds where the Queen likes to plant her favourite small plants and bulbs. Four *Malus tschonoskii* are planted at the centre of each of these beds. Large borders surround this central feature, where there is planted a variety of early-summer-flowering plants, including *Arum italicum* 'Marmoratum'; irises 'Melodrama', 'Amethyst Flame', 'Black Taffeta' and 'Jane Phillips'; peonies 'White Wings' and

Below left Yew hedges provide important winter structure.
Below right In spring, flowering trees and shrubs take centre stage: *Prunus* 'Shôgetsu' (right and left) flowers after *P.* 'Taihaku' (in the middle).

'Madame Emile Debatène'; lupins 'Blue Jacket' and 'Josephine', pulmonarias, *Euphorbia cyparissias*, hellebores, *Staphylea pinnata*, *Prunus glandulosa* 'Alba Plena', *Dicentra spectabilis*, *Rosa* 'Gloire de Dijon', *Asphodelus luteus*, *Paeonia officinalis* 'Rosea Plena', wallflowers, *Deutzia* 'Avalanche' and the tree peony, *Paeonia* × *lemonei* 'Souvenir de Maxime Cornu'.

In the yellow garden, a lawn leads to an area with narrow brick paths arranged in a pattern that divides the space into five beds. The outer four beds are planted with *Rosa* 'Norwich Union' and edged with the pale yellow *Helianthemum* 'Wisley Primrose'. The central bed has *Rosa* 'Moonlight', with *Santolina pinnata* subsp. *neapolitana* on the corners. Surrounding these are larger beds planted with yellow-flowering shrubs including *Genista aetnensis*, *Phlomis samia*, *Cytisus battandieri*, *Robinia pseudoacacia* 'Frisia', *Lupinus arboreus* 'Golden Spire', *Paeonia mlokosewitschii*, alchemilla and *Yucca filamentosa* 'Variegata'; *Rosa* 'Maigold' is trained over a small arch. The concentration of one-colour planting is very effective in a small space and yellow can be particularly successful for there are so many shrubs with yellow leaves to complement yellow flowers.

In the rose garden, a small central lawn is surrounded by several large beds, planted with old-fashioned roses such as 'Maiden's Blush', 'Celsiana', 'Conditorum', 'Du Maître d'Ecole', 'Duchesse de Montebello', 'Fantin-Latour', 'Louise Odier', 'Tuscany Superb', 'Isfahan', 'Madame Ernest Calvat', 'Hippolyte', 'The Bishop' and 'Coupe d'Hébé'. The Queen and I carefully chose the varieties to be what she and I had seen and loved. I wanted this garden to be abundant with roses. For repeat flowering we chose 'Comte de Chambord', 'Reine des Violettes' and 'Louise Odier'. For added interest I included a few herbaceous plants like *Hosta sieboldiana* var. *elegans* on either side of the seat at the base of the wooden arch. *Stachys byzantina*, *Helichrysum italicum*, *Phlomis italica* and *Salvia officinalis* 'Purpurascens' were planted to fill some of the gaps below the roses, together with various alliums and *Lilium regale*.

The herb and fruit garden has now become a miniature potager, with espaliered apples and pears, and various chaenomeles. Some beds are filled with alpine strawberries, some with lily-of-the-valley and others with herbs and flowers. Hyssop surrounds a central feature and creeping thymes spill over the paved paths.

Left In the rose garden, where grass contributes to the soft effect, *Rosa* 'Empress Josephine', *R.* 'Gloire de Guilan', *R.* 'Tour de Malakoff' and *R.* 'Baronne Adolph de Rothschild' flower profusely.

Far left, top to bottom *R.* 'Madame Lauriol de Barny' with purple *R.* 'Tuscany Superb'; cornflowers; clipped box shapes; and flowers of *Darmera peltata*.

Left, top Topiary box shapes make a centrepiece to the large octagon of grass which is at the centre of the whole garden; they are interplanted with *Rosa* 'Lavender Lassie', poppies and cornflowers, and surrounded by low box hedges. To the left, rambling rose 'Seagull' tumbles out of a tree.

Left, centre The rose garden is planted with an abundance of the old-fashioned roses loved by the Queen.

Left, bottom *Prunus* 'Taihaku', enclosed by yew hedges, at either side of the entrance to the gardens.

Below Plan of the garden of Château le Belvedere.

Pages 112–113 Spring and winter views of the lime walk, which runs the length of one side of the garden. The limes, *Tilia* x *euchlora*, are clipped very tightly, as is traditional in Belgium, trained on short bamboo canes and tied in with willow. Below are tulips, small daffodils and pulmonarias, mixed with muscari, scillas and primulas of different colours.

I didn't want too urban a feeling in any of these gardens, so I limited the use of brick paths. I chose a particularly pretty Dutch brick, mellow pink in colour and smaller than usual.

Beyond the carpet is a circular pool which was an existing feature. The planting around it is simple. Behind are cherries planted in a semicircle, with *Iris sibirica* beneath them; facing the pool is another semicircle of cherries at a slightly different radius. Between the cherry trees are hedges which radiate like the spokes of a wheel towards the pool. I wanted there to be a contrast between the central parterre pattern and the outer parts of the garden, with colour and pattern inside, and simplicity and peace outside – particularly around the pool.

I originally designed the garden nearly thirty years ago and I have been back nearly every year. The Queen and I constantly discuss it and I am currently updating the design of the gardens. When I originally designed the garden we had a limited palette of colour – fewer plants were available. It was then difficult to export plants to Belgium for there was no free movement of plants throughout Europe. Now I am adding to and changing the planting. And, supported by her creative energy and encouragement, I am also working on the park, planting trees and bulbs and designing grass walks with roses and many other features.

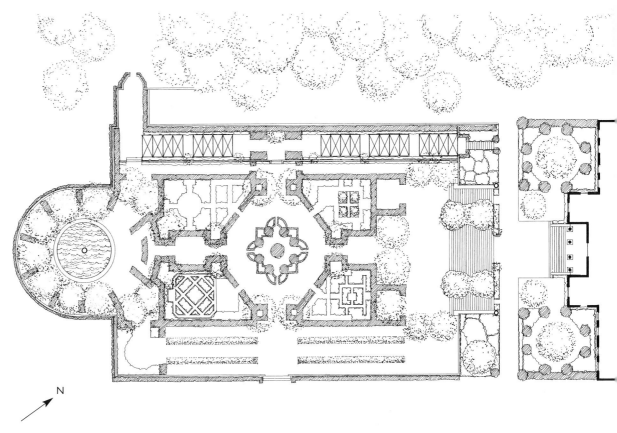

N

WOODLAND AND WATER

Gresgarth

During the first two years after we moved to Gresgarth in 1978, I was engaged in renovating the house and the birth of my second child. At that stage the garden was not my priority. This was probably no bad thing, for it gave me time to think about the particular challenges it presented (described on page 6), to observe and to soak in the atmosphere of the place.

I did however manage to clear some of the very oppressive woodland across the river – the Artle Beck – to the east and open views through the wooded valley in which the house sits. I subsequently also opened views to the charming park to the

north-west. There were some very good trees, planted seventy or eighty years ago, which I left. However, I cleared all the ponticum rhododendrons, the conifers and other evergreens throughout the garden. This, together with the loss of some of the old trees, opened the garden to the strong west wind. So the next task was to restore some shelter, by planting more trees in the park and hedges in the garden. In the park I planted several widely spaced holm oaks to break the force of the wind, terminating in a circle at the furthest end. I also added limes, chestnut and ash, as well as oak, beech, a small avenue of

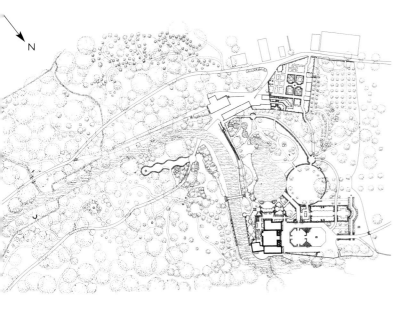

Left Plan of the garden.
Right A glimpse of the house from across the river is framed by *Magnolia denudata*.
Below, far left *Magnolia kobus*, above the Artle Beck.
Below, left The south-facing façade of the house, reflected in the lake. From the upper terrace two flights of steps lead down to the grass

octagons which form half-landings. Further steps lead to the lower terrace.
Below Steps lead from the house down to the river. On the right *Cotoneaster horizontalis* lines the steps, in front of white *Philadelphus* 'Beauclerk' and roses 'La Ville de Bruxelles', 'Henri Martin', 'Empress Josephine', 'Félicité Parmentier'. *Rosa* 'Alchymist' is trained around a wooden pyramid. The planting on the left includes *Acer corallinum* and *Rosa* 'Penelope' and in the foreground *Hosta fortunei* 'Francee' edges the border.

Liriodendron tulipifera and groups of *Populus balsamifera* in the wetter areas. Over the next few years I introduced yew hedges for shelter at a lower level and large borders like the lilac walk, all designed to moderate the wind. I also added a walk of pleached limes to create even more shelter for the herbaceous borders.

Today, as you arrive, a drive through the parkland leads to an entrance courtyard, a gravel sweep around a central lawn which is divided into two octagons, one surrounded by a yew hedge, the other with a large sculpture of a wild boar at its centre. The name Gresgarth means the place of the boar, and this particular boar is a copy of the Calydonian Boar, a Roman original now to be found in Florence. On arrival you hear the sound of the Artle Beck breaking over a weir at the back of the house. The noise of water is a constant and soothing feature throughout the garden.

On the eastern side, the Artle Beck divides the garden from the woodland beyond; below the house, to the south-west, the land drops down in a series of steps and terraces to a small lake which we reshaped. On the side of the house that faces the lake, I made the existing terrace much deeper and brought it

out, creating a terrace large enough to seat six people. I created beds along the walls of the house and others on the edge of the terrace so that the house is seen as though rising from a mass of plants and flowers. Later I designed additional formal terraces to continue the link to the lake. Two equal flights of steps lead from the top terrace to a transitional terrace designed as two octagons of grass, inspired by a Lutyens design that I had seen at Great Dixter, Christopher Lloyd's garden in Sussex. From these octagons, two shorter flights lead down to a lower terrace which runs to the water's edge. As these terraces are near the house, it was important that they should have structural planting to provide winter interest, so I planted large box balls and other topiary shapes, as well as roses 'Felicia' and 'Comte de Chambord'. The lower terrace is planted with a variety of herbaceous plants: *Hesperis matronalis* var. *albiflora*, *Allium nigrum*, white campanulas, *Anthericum liliago* and *Thalictrum delavayi* 'Album' are planted amongst *Rosa* 'Yvonne Rabier', the only white shrub rose I can grow successfully. The wall behind is clad with *R.* 'Mrs Herbert R. Stevens', *Clematis*

'Henryi', C. 'Alba Luxurians' and *Wisteria venusta*. Two small arbours built at the water's edge on either side, looking out over the lake, are covered with *R.* 'Rambling Rector'.

On the west side of these terraces I planted a double yew hedge. This forms a narrow walk that links the entrance garden to the small lake. It was the first of a series of enclosures I made on the west side of the house to provide very necessary shelter. Now we have here a series of gardens surrounded by yew hedges: they include a wildflower garden, so called because it has been colonized by wild orchids and harebells; and a large circular lawn, planted with an inner circle of late-flowering *Prunus* 'Okumiyako', a simple and peaceful feature.

The part of the garden I designed most recently comprises three different herbaceous gardens. The first is a small square garden with a wonderful paving designed by Maggie Howarth for us: it features our interests in architecture and in Italy, and includes the four zodiacs of the family birthdays linked by the Milky Way. The borders are planted with herbaceous plants in various shades of yellow, orange, red and burgundy, including the tawny flowers of *Helenium* 'Moerheim Beauty' and *H.* 'Rubinkuppel', the orange *Papaver rupifragum*, the paler *P. orientale* 'Juliane', *Rosa* 'Frensham', *Verbascum chaixii* 'Cotswold Queen' and *V.* 'Royal Highland', underplanted with *Heuchera* 'Stormy Seas', orange polyanthus and helianthemums in every shade from tawny brown to bright orange. The richness is softened by grasses such as *Deschampsia cespitosa* 'Goldschleier', *Stipa arundinacea* and *Carex elata* 'Aurea'.

From the square you walk on to a lawn flanked by herbaceous borders where the flowers are all shades of blue, mauve and pink, with touches of burgundy. Four *Cotinus coggygria* 'Royal Purple'

Left A Coalbrookdale cast-iron seat surrounded by *Rosa* 'Empress Josephine', with 'May Queen' behind on the wall and 'Charles Austin' in front of dark delphinium 'Faust', on the river side of the lower terrace. Some pretty miniature hurdles made for me of cleft oak hold back *Nepeta racemosa* 'Walker's Low', backed by *Dicentra formosa* 'Alba' and Gallica rose 'Cardinal de Richelieu'.
Right The lake side of the lower terrace. The paving slabs are set in a geometric pattern of small black cobbles. On either side of the terrace, *Pyrus salicifolia* 'Pendula' arches over *Hebe subalpina* and tiered box. On the upper terrace sits a pillar sundial designed by my husband, Mark.

Top *Prunus* 'Shirofugen' in early May, underplanted with *Narcissus* 'Dove Wings'.
Above The pink flowers of *Malus floribunda* and a very old variety of prunus contrast with the red-painted uprights and finials of the bridge.
Opposite The upper terrace on the west side of the house. Around the sitting area standard *Prunus lusitanica* rises above box platforms, while *Allium cristophii* is contained in a box parterre. Rosa Mundi flowers in the foreground, *Rosa* 'Reine des Violettes' at the far end of the terrace and 'Ispahan' on the corner of the house.

are planted at the back of the borders at regular intervals. The flowering season starts with clumps of *Tulipa* 'Queen of Night' underplanted with pansies Antique Pink shades, followed by *Phlox carolina*, early campanulas, *Hesperis matronalis*, *Geranium* 'Johnson's Blue' and *G. psilostemon*. Delphiniums, *Phlox paniculata* 'Cool of the Evening' and 'Blue Paradise' follow on, with *Monarda* 'Fishes' ('Pisces') and 'Ruby Glow'. *Nepeta grandiflora* 'Bramdean', one of my favourites, grows so enthusiastically that I have had to move it back from the edge of the border to the second row. *Thalictrum rochebruneanum*, *T. delavayi* 'Hewitt's Double' and *Verbena bonariensis* are allowed to seed at will. The last plants to flower are asters of various shades, starting with *Aster amellus* 'King George', *A.* × *frikartii* 'Mönch' and *A. laevis* 'Calliope', its mahogany stems rising through *Stipa calamagrostis* and other grasses.

At the end of the borders, across a small path, you enter the third enclosure, which is planted with white *Phlox paniculata* 'Mount Fuji', *Verbascum* × *hybridum* 'Snow Maiden', *Miscanthus sinensis* 'Yakushima Dwarf', *M. s.* 'Morning Light', and *Calamagrostis brachytricha*. *Monarda* 'Snow Queen' flowers from July to September, as do *Peucedanum ostruthium* 'Daphnis' and *Selinum tenuifolium*.

The yew hedges not only shelter the garden from the west wind but also hide the path that runs all the way from the herbaceous borders to the vegetable garden on the western boundary.

When we arrived, the old walled vegetable garden was used for growing Christmas trees and was colonized by mare's-tail. With some effort all the perennial weeds were eradicated, and then we subdivided the area with paths and made beds for vegetables and cut flowers. Some of the beds are edged in box, and all are finished with the Victorian rope-edge tile. It has taken a long time to improve the heavy soil, but after years of double-digging and incorporating plenty of compost and well-rotted manure, it now produces a fine crop of vegetables and fruit.

Below the house to the east, the garden sloped down to the river. In order to raise the riverside level and make a plateau to connect with the front lower terrace, I added another elongated octagon with bigger borders and gravel octagons on either side. To continue the structural effect of the terraces, I planted buttresses of yew, clipped in a castellated shape, to match the architectural style of the house and to add some interest to an otherwise dull wall. These yew hedges are mirrored by counterparts on the far side of the river. *Rosa* 'New Dawn' is planted on both sides all the way between the structures. The tumbling roses soften the topiary and partly cover the wall. Looking out over the river is an octagonal metal arbour which, in summer, is also covered with roses.

Right, above In the vegetable garden, sweet peas will shortly flower from the hazel obelisks. The wicker cloches are more decorative than functional, though they do protect young plants from early frosts.

Right, below A white and blue border on the lower terrace including white rose 'Climbing Iceberg' and tall blue *Delphinium* 'Faust', with white *Allium nigrum* and silver-leaved artemisias and other plants in the foreground.

Opposite, main picture Maggie Howarth's paving design for the orange and red garden shows an olive tree – representing Italy, and a symbol for me – and a temple – representing architecture and a symbol for my husband – and, beyond, the wind with puffy cheeks is at the entrance to the blue and pink herbaceous borders. The planting includes *Phlomis* 'Lloyd's Variety' and *Euphorbia dulcis* 'Chameleon' on either side of the entrance. Orange helianthemums, *Geum* 'Lady Strathallen' and *Potentilla* 'William Robinson' are followed by Oriental poppies in all shades from red to orange, *Hemerocallis*, *Verbascum chaixii* 'Cotswold Queen', *Achillea* 'Walther Funke', *Rudbeckia*, *Helenium* 'Rubinzwerg', *Digitalis feruginea*, *Crocosmia* and *Coreopsis*. Various grasses are planted to soften the bright colours. Beyond, the blue, mauve and pink borders are planted with delphiniums, monardas, *Geranium psilostemon* and *Nepeta* among an enormous variety of other herbaceous plants and grasses.

Opposite, far right

Top Sweet peas *Lathyrus belinensis* from Turkey trained over a wigwam of hazel twigs in a pot.

Centre Rows of leafy produce in the vegetable garden.

Bottom The peerless David Sayer, our head gardener.

Following the path nearest the house along the river there is a series of spring borders where I planted hellebores and small evergreen azaleas and rhododendrons underplanted with spring woodland plants and bulbs. Varieties of trillium, pulmonarias, anemones, scillas, erythroniums and primulas fill the gaps. At the head of the lake, I designed several small ponds linked by stone steps. The borders around them are for a late May display and are planted with *Meconopsis grandis*, *M. regia*, *M. napaulensis*, *Primula florindae*, *P. pulverulenta*, *P.p.* Bartley hybrids and *P. candelabra* 'Posford White', a collection of *Iris laevigata* from Japan, *Lysimachia clethroides,* and small willows, azaleas and other shrubs, which together create a colourful damp garden.

Midway along the riverside path, a wood bridge with red-lacquered posts takes you across the river to a woodland; an avenue of *Malus hupehensis* leads into it. It is planted with a variety of sorbus, birch, stewartias, styrax, magnolias and a collection of hamamelis to which I am still adding. When we began to clear the ground there was evidence of shrub borders and I deduced that there must once have been a rhododendron garden here: I found the edges of the borders as well as some of the original rhododendrons which had been smothered by other plants. So I dug the borders and reinstated this part of the garden, adding more *Rhododendron vaseyi*, *R.* 'Pink Pearl', *R.* 'Silver Slipper', *R.* 'Mrs A.T. de la Mare', *R.* 'Mrs Charles E. Pearson', *R.* 'Sweet Simplicity', *R.* Winsome Group, *Oemleria cerasiformis*, *Prunus yedoensis*, *Rosa roxburghii*, *Magnolia hypoleuca*, *Salix fargesii*, *Meliosma* and many other plants. This side of the valley is very cold, because of the wind and because the river brings down cold air with it. So I planted a serpentine beech hedge, which shelters the borders as well as making an interesting feature.

Over the years I have slowly opened up the wood. I took out sycamores and scrubby trees and replaced them with rare specimens, including acers, oaks, stewartias and magnolias. That process continues – I have planted more than 3000 new trees and shrubs in the woods on the two sides of the river. I have also introduced sculpture, some antique and some modern, as eye-catchers to lead one further on.

Gresgarth is now visually very different from other English gardens – perhaps because I brought to the English countryside my Italian background and preferences.

A misty morning early summer view of the damp border surrounding the pools that feed the lake. The magical blue *Meconopsis* × *sheldonii* dominates the scene, rising out of a sea of wild garlic punctuated by *Darmera peltata*. Nearby, *Osmunda regalis* unfurls, while *Hosta fortunei* 'Francee' spreads its cream-edged leaves. In the distance, *Rhododendron* 'Sylphides' and *R. augustinii* 'Werrington' bring more colour to the pond borders.

OASIS IN THE WILDERNESS
Las Navas

The Spanish countryside surrounding Las Navas, near the city of Toledo, was the key to my design of this garden. The house is on high ground, surrounded by scrub, and the land around it originally sloped quite steeply away down the hill. The landscape is one of severe beauty – a flat plain of deep earth colours against a backdrop of far-off hills. It is dramatic, almost hostile, and cannot be ignored, so it was important that the garden should in a sense acknowledge the landscape and work with it rather than against it.

Of course a garden has also to be separate from the landscape, and should always relate to the house. To achieve this at Las Navas I first had to make a large flat area surrounding the house to accommodate the garden. So I raised the land in front of the house and built a wall 2.5 metres (8 feet) high round three sides of the property; this would support and contain the new garden like ramparts, giving it the fitting aspect of a desert fortress. Then, to integrate the property into the farther landscape, on the land directly beneath the walls I planted many olive trees,

underplanting them with lavenders in shades of blue, pink and white, as well as a huge variety of irises; these have spread naturally and look beautiful with the olives. At the entrance I designed a geometric pattern of olive trees underplanted – in segments – with more lavender in white, mauve, blue and dark blue, and blocks of irises such as *Iris* 'Elvinhall' and *I.* 'Focus'. Thus there is a graceful transition from the wild landscape to the deliberately planted but natural-looking olive trees, lavender and irises and then to their

Right In the entrance courtyard, paved with cobbles, a well and fountain surrounded by four cypresses form a centrepiece. The fountain cools the air as well as making a pleasant sound. *Iris* 'Out Yonder' is planted with lavender at the base of the cypress trees.

Far right, from top to bottom Pale blue irises below the wall amongst lavender and olive trees; *Iris* 'Fantastic Voyage' prettily combined with *Rosa* 'Graham Thomas'; a design for iron gates; a modern sculpture positioned as an eye-catcher, with the mighty view beyond; a detail of the ironwork for another pair of gates.

Below The cascade at Las Navas was inspired by one at the Villa Lante in Italy. This modern version uses concrete with pebbles set into it for the steps, and box to imitate the shapes at the Villa Lante.

Above High retaining walls rise like ramparts from the plain to support and contain the garden round the house.

Below On the east side of the house, ceanothus and roses frame a view of a covered veranda which looks out across a lawn simply furnished with solid blocks of yew hedge. Tall cypresses in a box-edged bed separate the lawn from the entrance to the swimming pool beyond.

formally planted counterparts at the threshold of the garden.

At the entrance I designed a drive, paved with granite setts, which divides into two, each section curving upwards into the large arrival courtyard. From here openings through cypress hedges to the west and east lead you to the gardens surrounding the house. I designed these as a series of separate areas or garden rooms, and I enclosed each with hedges of cypress, pittosporum or, in some cases, large borders, to give the impression that the house was emerging from a sea of green. Each garden is different in design and plant colour. The owner, who takes great pride in the garden, planted them with me.

The arrival court is spacious and elegant; a pool and fountain with cypresses at the four corners form a centrepiece. There are generous borders against the house and narrow borders on either side of the courtyard along the cypress hedges. To the west, outside the drawing room, is a yellow garden, simple in design – a rectangular lawn with borders planted mainly with roses, including, on the house, *Rosa* 'Desprez à Fleurs Jaunes', and silver-leaved and yellow shrubs with a few blue touches, such as phlomis, halimiocistus, *Myrtus apiculata* 'Glanleam Gold',

Perovskia 'Blue Spire', *Asphodelus luteus* and agapanthus.

The owners also wanted a shady space in which to sit and eat, so when I designed the ramparts I extended them outwards at two points – from the yellow garden and, further along, from the white garden. This not only created large bays at ground level where cars could be parked out of sight, but also allowed me to make a large paved terrace off the yellow garden. Here I designed a wooden pergola, which is covered with roses: 'Aimée Vibert', 'Paul's Lemon Pillar' and 'Bobbie James'. The whole terrace is surrounded by a rosemary hedge and is a lovely place to sit, with a wonderful view over the plain.

Beyond the yellow garden is a small, simple, square blue and silver garden, where four *Elaeagnus angustifolia*, grown as trees, are the main feature; not only do they have beautiful silver leaves, but they are also highly scented when in flower. Through a hedge of *Pittosporum tobira*, you are led down steps into the delicate, silver-toned, white garden, which is paved with cobbles. Leading off it is a scented garden on the extended ramparts. The white garden is cool and elegant, planted with white *Rosa* 'Iceberg' and silver-leaved shrubs; at the centre is a

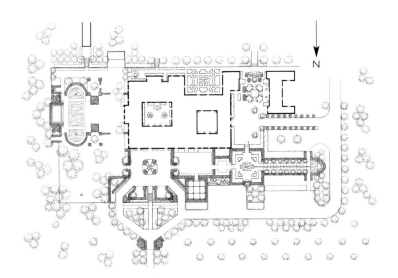

Above Plan of the garden.
Below The centrepiece of the cobblestoned white garden is a cross-shaped pool where water lilies and arum lilies surround a statue of a nymph blowing water through a horn. From the pool a narrow channel takes the water to the top of the cascade. The garden is surrounded by a hedge of *Pittosporum tobira*. In the corners, stepped box-edged beds contain *Rosa* 'Iceberg' with *Elaeagnus angustifolia* and other silver-leaved plants such as *Salvia lavandulifolia*, *Ballota pseudodictamnus* and *Potentilla fruticosa* 'Abbotswood'.

cruciform pool with a statue of a nymph blowing a horn, through which water falls. The water runs through a rill to a set of shallow steps which form a cascade – the most dramatic feature of this garden. These are an interpretation of those at Villa Lante in Italy, and have a contemporary, formal elegance. I used local cobble-stones set in concrete and, either side of the rill, box clipped to represent the fish-like shapes at Villa Lante. The cascade comes to rest in a shallow semicircular pool. Flanking the steps are olive trees, with red *Rosa* 'Scharlachght' rambling through them, underplanted with lavender and the purple *Iris germanica*. The foliage here, with its tones of grey and silver-green, gives the scene a misty, ethereal feel, the olives rising like wraiths.

From the white garden you pass through a small Moorish-style iron gate and cross an open terrace to an area that links the guest house to the main house. Outside the guest house is a large iron pergola, also of Moorish inspiration, which I planted with *Rosa* 'Guinée' and *R.* 'Madame Grégoire Staechelin', set in four flat beds of box whose solidity visually anchors the pergola.

East of the entrance courtyard, through the cypress hedge, is a large lawn, with towering umbrella pines and a dramatic view of the surrounding countryside. The area is a deliberately impressive setting to display the owners' contemporary sculpture collection. Beyond this is the swimming pool, visually separated by two large square beds, edged with box hedges each containing five cypresses. There are large beds of the yellow rose 'Graham Thomas' and behind that, against the wall, a long border of *Rosa* 'Iceberg' and *Iris* 'Fantastic Voyage' with terracotta pots planted with white petunias placed along the border at regular intervals to break up the length of the wall.

In this part of Spain the climate is extreme, the summers very hot and winters extremely cold, so tender plants like orange trees and jasmine can't survive; and water is scarce, though reservoirs on the property helped maintain hedges and trees in the first years. But now, five years later, with the cultivated areas around the house well established, the gardens seem to rise like a fortified oasis from the dusty wilderness beyond.

Left, from top to bottom Irises and roses planted informally along the drive; olive trees underplanted with blue, pink and white lavender to soften the landscape; a pergola supporting climbing roses shelters a seating area on a terrace formed by buttresses that jut out from the ramparts.
Right The planting around the terraces at the edge of the garden includes olive trees, *Rosa* 'Zéphirine Drouhin', *Phlomis fruticosa*, *Iris* 'Out Yonder', *Centranthus ruber* and *C.r.* 'Albus'.
Pages 130–131 A sublime view, framed by pergola columns and cypresses, over the informally planted outer garden to the plain and the distant hills. *Cistus × purpureus* in the foreground and *Rosa* 'White Bells' grow over the wall below the cypresses.

A TROPICAL GARDEN
A Garden in Barbados

This lush, tropical garden on the Caribbean coast of the island of Barbados surrounds a house of coral stone. Compact, with two wings, it is airy and light, and has exposed beams, gingerbread – or fretwork – decoration and a shingled roof. In 1996 the owners bought a neighbouring plot, which slopes sharply downhill, and in the centre of the plot was a large chasm where a previous owner had begun and then abandoned the building of a house. There were a few good mahogany trees, and a mango, but it had been stripped of most of its topsoil and looked desolate. As well as improving the land and making a garden, the owners wanted me to find a good site for a new building that was to be a large drawing room, to link it with the existing main house above it, and to find a suitable place for a tennis court and a pavilion, and also a private drive which would lead directly to my clients' quarters.

Once I had found a position for the new room, the key to the design was to connect the main house with the new building and to set the garden around it. A tropical garden will, of necessity, be mainly informal because plants are so lush and growth so rapid, but a formal design is more fitting for a link

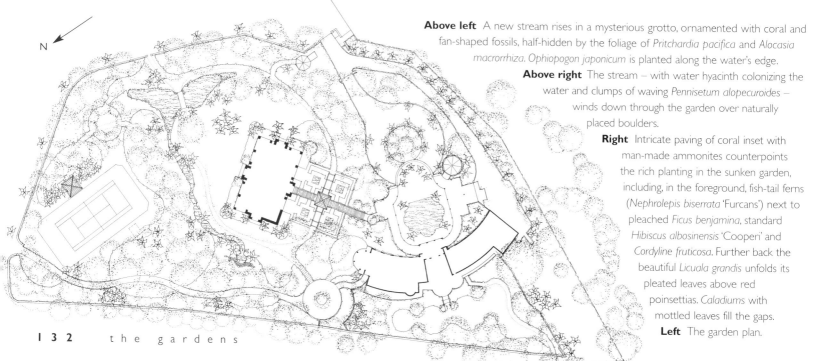

Above left A new stream rises in a mysterious grotto, ornamented with coral and fan-shaped fossils, half-hidden by the foliage of *Pritchardia pacifica* and *Alocasia macrorrhiza*. *Ophiopogon japonicum* is planted along the water's edge.

Above right The stream – with water hyacinth colonizing the water and clumps of waving *Pennisetum alopecuroides* – winds down through the garden over naturally placed boulders.

Right Intricate paving of coral inset with man-made ammonites counterpoints the rich planting in the sunken garden, including, in the foreground, fish-tail ferns (*Nephrolepis biserrata* 'Furcans') next to pleached *Ficus benjamina*, standard *Hibiscus albosinensis* 'Cooperi' and *Cordyline fruticosa*. Further back the beautiful *Licuala grandis* unfolds its pleated leaves above red poinsettias. *Caladiums* with mottled leaves fill the gaps.

Left The garden plan.

N

Far left above and below, and middle In the sunken garden that links the new building (called the Great Room) with the original house, plant growth is so sumptuous and exuberant that it almost obscures the formality of the geometric layout, with its four garden rooms, each with a central pool. The garden is enclosed by pleached *Ficus benjamina*; this and the other rich greens from the contrasting foliage of *Licuala* palms, fishtail ferns and giant crinums serve as a background to the bright reds of the *Cordyline fruticosa* and poinsettias. The paler peachy pinks of the scented trumpets of *Brugmansia x candida* 'Blush' mix well with the 'white- and red-varigated caladiums below. *Strongylodon macrobotrys* (the jade vine) winds up the handsome wooden columns and festoons the slatted roof of the pergola. *Pittosporum cuneatum* 'Nanum Variegatum' marks the edges of the beds.

Left A path leading to the Great Room passes among Christmas palms (*Veitchia merrillii*) and variegated giant crinums (*Crinum japonicum* 'Variegatum'). Lower down are small variegated grasses (*Ophiopogon* 'Kijimafukiduma'). Red acalypha can be glimpsed in the distance.

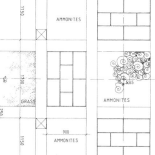

Clockwise from left I constructed the grotto myself, with the help of local workers; a plan of the paving scheme used in the formal sunken gardens; the beach spider lily (*Hymenocallis littoralis*); dark pink *Allamanda blanchetii*; *Petrea volubilis*; the tennis-court pavilion, designed to reflect the Bajan architecture of the house, with pink bougainvillea planted to partly disguise the court's netting; the white *Mussaenda philippica* 'Aurorae' with the trumpets of *Brugmansia* x *candida* 'Ecuador Pink'; the hardwood and bamboo bridge crosses the narrow pool like the body of a butterfly, the wings of water widening on either side; a vibrant *Heliconia nickeriensis*.

between man-made structures, so I designed a square, sunken garden crossed by a cruciform wooden pergola. Geometrically formal, it is divided into four smaller garden rooms, the whole surrounded by pleached *Ficus benjamina* trees. In each garden there is a pool of water planted with water lilies, and bordered with tropical plants like datura (*Brugmansia*) and *Murraya paniculata* and, for colour, red cordylines. Shafts of light enter and there is a romantic contrast of light and shade between the pergola, the pleached fig and the open spaces. The covered pergola is inspired by the airy, plantation architecture of the house, with narrow columns supporting a sloping, shingled roof; the columns are festooned with the jade vine (*Strongylodon macrobotrys*). One crosspiece links the new room – known as the Great Room – with the upper level of the main house; the other leads you out to the two other main features of the garden design: on one side the tropical walk, on the other the stream.

The Great Room is surrounded with borders and a lawn which slopes gently down the hill. At the four corners of the room, I brought the beds out into semicircles and planted three royal palms (*Roystonea regia*) in each, to anchor the room in the landscape. Fan palms (*Pritchardia pacifica*) are planted round the doors which lead out on to the lawn to the north and south. In the borders I used plants to create different groups of colour: in one border I planted a *Graptophyllum pictum*, shaded pink, to combine with pink bougainvillea and pink *Hibiscus rosa-sinensis*; in another I combined *Thunbergia erecta* and *T. grandiflora* with *Vitex agnus-castus* – all of different shades of blue. Some of the borders are edged with the Boston fern (*Nephrolepsis exaltata* 'Bostoniensis'), a dark blue plumbago which in Barbados grows as a low shrub, and the scented carissa, which looks very much like a large-flowered jasmine.

A stream is a natural element in an informal, sloping garden, and so on one side of the garden I created a stream that appears to rise from a spring in a grotto tucked into the hill on the same level and to the east of the new Great Room. From the grotto, the stream flows down the length of the garden, over small cascades and through a series of small pools, ending in a larger, butterfly-shaped pool at the bottom of the site, in which there are locally quarried rocks made of coral stone.

I decided to try and construct the grotto myself – with the help of a very willing local team, and using some beautiful pieces of coral stone and fossils that we found locally. The course of the stream was then dug and its bed lined with Gunnite, a waterproof cement which is sprayed on to a base of stones and netting. To make the stream look natural, stones were carefully placed on the edges and on the small cascade

steps, and on the banks I arranged some groups of very large stones, while elsewhere I left the grass to grow to the water's edge. More palms follow the meandering of the stream down the garden, and the traveller's palm (*Ravenala madagascariensis*) was planted above the grotto. Around it I planted large-leaved plants like philodendron, alocasias and *Ficus lyrata*, as well as the banana tree (*Musa acuminata* 'Dwarf Cavendish'). I planted short ornamental grasses such as leriope at the edge of the grotto. Along the river edge, to give a sense of movement, I used other clumps of grasses of different heights. The tall *Cyperus papyrus* is planted in the water.

We designed two bridges: one, inspired by a visit to Japan, a simple, unobtrusive, yet quite chunky, slab of concrete treated to look like coral stone, and another which appears to be the body of the butterfly, constructed in hardwood and bamboo.

The locally found fossils and coral were the inspiration for the many steps and winding paths we created in the garden. I used coral because it loses its whiteness soon after it is laid; a moss often then grows on it, which softens the effect of the stone. To break up the monotony of uninterrupted coral, and to echo the real fossils found in the garden, we inset pretty artificial ammonites in different designs, which we had found in England.

Echoing the curved route of the stream, on the other side of the Great Room (the west side) and in the shade of some existing mature trees, I created a tropical woodland walk which begins as you leave the formal garden, and which also curves down to the butterfly pond. Shady, leafy and enclosed, it is planted with bold-leaved tropical plants of different textures in shades of green, red and yellow and is now known as the Jungle Walk. There are gingers (*Alpinia purpurata* and *A. zerumbet*) and also the bird's nest fern (*Asplenium nidus*), datura, mussaenda (a large shrub with big clusters of white or pink flowers), clumps of *Crinum moorei*, heliconia and groups of *Hibiscus* 'La France', *H.* 'Opalescent Pink' and *H.* 'Cooperi' – this last being a variegated hibiscus with red flowers. I planted as groundcover spider lilies (*Hymenocallis littoralis*), pilea and syngonium, as well as setcreasea, a green succulent groundcover, and rhoeo, which has a green leaf with a red underside. I also included white begonia, dracaena and dieffenbachia.

Here, as in the rest of the garden, I used trees and palms I found in local nurseries, because it is legally difficult to import plants into Barbados. I planted mahogany (*Swietenia mahogani*) and other large trees like pride of India (*Peltophorum ferrugineum*), the pink *Cassia jervanica*, pride of Barbados (*Caesalpinia pulcherrima*), and *Cochlospermum vitifolium,* a lovely tree with huge yellow pompon flowers; also the African tulip tree (*Spathodea campanulata*), the Spanish ash (*Lonchocarpus violaceus*) and the mango (*Mangifera indica*), as well as the white-flowered *Bauhinia acuminata*. The palms known locally as the golden palm, the royal palm, the cabbage palm (*Roystonea oleracea*), the queen palm and the red-fruited Christmas palm (*Veitchia merrillii*) were available in abundance.

I decided to site the tennis court, with its north–south orientation, on a fairly large section of ground on the lowest part of the site, where it could be screened by trees and landscaping – the stream runs through a small valley and the land, rising beyond it before dropping down again, hides the court. To reach the court, the path crosses the stream by a simple bridge and goes up through a tropical orchard of mango, sapodilla, Barbados cherry, carambola, star fruit and ackee. This orchard path then curves round to the new tennis pavilion, which is built in Bajan (Barbadian) style and planted with jasmine and white-flowering *Euphorbia leucocephala*, known as 'Snow in the Mountains'; this grows to over 1 metre (3 feet) high, and is covered with tiny white flowers at Christmas time. I also planted white spatoglossis with cestrum growing through it, and *Philodendron melinonii* at the corners. The netting surrounding the tennis court is covered with bougainvillea, and *Ficus benjamina* is planted on the corners to help to shade the court. Just beyond is the new drive, which winds its way through the trees to the private apartments.

I was very lucky because the contractor I worked with here was very reliable and has become a good friend – and he also has a very good nursery. Because of my interest he has grown many plants from seed and imported others, so guaranteeing many rare plants for this garden. Other local nurseries are also good and are trying hard to grow unusual plants and trees.

I had never designed a tropical garden before, so it was a terrific challenge and very exciting, particularly since the clients gave me complete freedom. I did an immense amount of research, and in Barbados I immersed myself in the vegetation and the landscape, walking the hills and visiting many gardens and nurseries. I learnt that tropical gardening is very different from gardening either in England or in the Mediterranean. In Barbados there is a rainy season of several months, and though it is drier than some other tropical islands, the heat and humidity are intense. The rain, combined with humidity and regular irrigation, encourages the plants to grow all the time, and at terrific speed.

Tropical plants have such fantastic shapes and wonderful colours – the greens in particular are very dominant, and strong plants that I would never normally use, such as dracaena, dieffenbachia, aglaonema, acalypha and caladium, look marvellous if planted in bold groups and in good colour combinations. However, though so colourful, plants in tropical gardens do not flower as abundantly – too much of their energy is going into the fantastically rapid growth. Bougainvillea, for example, flowers profusely if planted in dry conditions but if given a lush and regularly watered bed will send out long green shoots with very small panicles of flowers on the tips. I therefore learnt to take great account of leaf colour as well as flower colour. I used plants like codiaeum, with its different-shaped leaves of russet, green and yellow, and cordyline, which can either be green, russet or pink or in variegated shades, and pandanus, which is large and spiky. Other plants have spots, or are mottled, edged or variegated. *Caladium*, for example, comes in green or combinations of green, white and red; philodendrons, unloved in England, are splendid in the tropics because they climb through trees. *Calathea* used as a mass is spectacular, as is graptophyllum, which comes in subtle, wonderful shades and which I have planted in those borders where I have concentrated on mixing colour.

Scent, too, is different in the tropics: it is only released when the temperature falls in the evening, and then only by those plants and trees with a naturally strong perfume, like ylang-ylang (*Cananga odorata*), the white-flowered frangipani *Plumeria obtusa* 'Singapore' and the night-scented *Cestrum nocturnum*. The subtle fragrance of jasmine, for example, is lost.

Throughout this garden there is rhythm and change; a contrast of light, shade and colour. There is the restless sound of the glittering water flowing down one side of the garden, the open expanse of the lawn and the contrast with the dark secrets and bold texture of the jungle walk. The contrast between night and day, between the power of the heat of the day and the softness of the evenings when all the scents are released, is very strong and makes the entire garden a very sensual place. And everywhere there is the interplay of shadow and light. What I love about this garden, which I consciously planned, is the strong contrast between light and dark – dark areas with shafts of light into open spaces, whether in the formality of the sunken garden or the jungle-like wildness of the paths beneath the trees. I think of this garden as quite an achievement, and it grew so fast as to be almost miraculous – in two years it had reached near-maturity.

Right above A view between the royal palms (*Roystonea regia*), across a gently sloping lawn towards the Great Room. A *Plumeria rubra* near the stream exudes the most delicate but powerful scent, particularly near the water.
Right below The delicate *Licuala grandis,* with elegantly pleated leaves, is planted at the entrance to each pool garden. Here it can be seen below the rare jade vine (*Strongylodon macrobotrys*). The petrol-blue racemes can droop to the ground and are a sight to remember.

A GREAT ESTATE

Eaton Hall

In 1990, the Duke and Duchess of Westminster asked me to redesign the gardens at Eaton Hall because they were building a new house – the fifth to be built on the site since the seventeenth century. I was called in at the very

beginning of the project, which was interesting for me because I worked with the architect, Sir Hugh Casson, as well as John Stefanidis, who was doing the interior design. The challenge was to make a garden that related to an historical past but that, at the same time, worked in a modern context with a new house.

In terms of its historical influence, Alfred Waterhouse's High Victorian Gothic palace of the 1870s – the third house – was perhaps the most important. Waterhouse remodelled the garden front, building large, sloping terraces, descending to elaborate parterres designed by the Victorian garden designer William Andrews Nesfield in about 1851. In 1911, the Arts and Crafts architect Detmar Blow remodelled much of the garden.

At first I was overwhelmed by the grandeur of the whole setting – the size of the terraces, the large enclosures, the sheer extent of an 85-acre garden. The most important challenge was to relate the new Hall, which is small compared with its predecessors, to its grand

Above A view of the gardens and park from above, showing the rose gardens and the redesigned canal.

Left Two huge statues are a focal point at the centre of the lawns which divide the four rose gardens. *Rosa* 'Bonica' in the foreground is planted in the central bed of the pink rose garden. Beyond is a view of the dark burgundies and purple shades of the crimson and purple rose garden. The trellis pyramids amid the spires of purple and paler mauve delphiniums are mixed with dark pink clematis and burgundy roses.

Pages 142–3 Four aspects of the rose gardens, each with a central bed and yew topiary of different shapes. Clockwise from top left: roses 'Iceberg' and 'Yvonne Rabier' with *Lavandula angustifolia* 'Alba', in the white garden; the pink garden, with roses 'Jacques Cartier', 'Baronne Adolph de Rothschild', 'Fantin-Latour', 'Old Pink Moss' and 'Ispilanté'; the yellow garden with, at the centre, roses 'Buff Beauty' surrounded by *Helianthemum* 'Wisley Primrose', and in the outer beds, roses 'The Pilgrim', 'Graham Thomas' and 'Mrs Oakley Fisher', *Thalictrum flavum* at the back and *Hosta* 'Aureomarginata'; the crimson and mauve garden, with 'L. D. Braithwaite' roses *en masse* at the centre with 'Tuscany Superb' and *Clematis* 'Hagley Hybrid', *Salvia nemorosa* 'Amethyst' and *Campanula lactiflora* 'Loddon Anna', and in the outer beds, *Eremurus stenophyllus* rising above the roses, forming an interesting contrast to the purple hues of the other flowers.

surroundings, without making the house seem even more modest in comparison. This necessitated a strong, authoritative design for the top terrace, the area of the garden immediately outside the house and its narrow new upper terrace. The question was how to create a garden that would act as a transition between the new house and the existing buildings, including the monumental church tower to the north-west – a surviving part of the old building and three times taller than the house. I also needed to relate the gardens of the house to the other Victorian terraces and the vast landscape around Eaton Hall, which stretched down to the River Dee in the distance.

I designed very deep herbaceous borders around the balustrade and around the house, to help to anchor it and its upper stone terrace in the landscape. For added emphasis, I planted two double rows of pleached limes, which form a structural link between the curved stone steps that come down from the upper terrace and the two flights of steps that lead down towards the Rose Garden. The lines of limes give height and weight to the top garden as well as directing the way to the Rose Garden beyond. They also divide the area in front of the house into three parts: there is a central plain lawn and, on either side, a modern parterre in the form of quatrefoil plats, the design cut out of the grass. A further walk of pleached limes leading round the north and west edge of the terrace to a side gate adds height to the planting below the church tower, creates a design link between tower and house and helps correct the

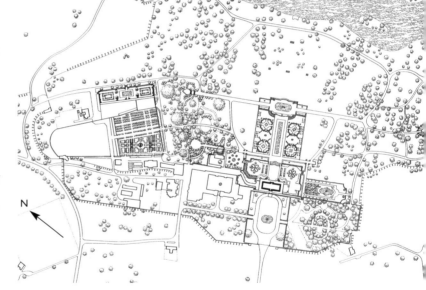

Above On the top terrace is a modern interpretation of a traditional parterre: a quatrefoil pattern cut out of grass on either side of a central expanse of lawn.

Left In the Dragon Fountain Garden, I redesigned Nesfield's Victorian parterre. One of the spring schemes is a mixture of tulips – red 'Landseadel's Supreme' and dark burgundy 'Queen of Night' – with pansies at the edges. The perennial evergreen *Bergenia* 'Silberlicht' decorates the base of the urn.

Right This plan shows the vast area of terraces and gardens in relation to the compact size of the house.

architectural disparity between the two.

In the south and west corner of the terrace there is a smaller, more intimate area which was to be used by the family, so there I designed a paved area for sitting out, with large borders almost enclosing it. Opposite it I brought the border back in from the south boundary and planted a *Prunus* 'Shirotae' to act as a focal point from the sitting area. With a matching planting a little to the south it marks the edges of a U-shaped bay which projects from the upper terrace, leading the eye to the Dragon Fountain Garden, where the U shape is echoed in the patterning, thus bringing the upper terrace into the wider garden.

The planting on the top terrace is designed to look good all year. I planted shrubs, trees and bulbs to flower in succession through the seasons in tones of predominantly pink, blue and buff to complement the pale pink stone of the building. Flowering cherries flank the steps leading down to the path to the Dragon Fountain Garden to the south, and, to give height, *Pyrus salicifolia* 'Pendula' is spaced regularly in the large borders along the edge of the terrace. Silver plants and hostas give an evergreen structure and Hybrid Musk roses are planted at intervals.

Two flights of steps lead down to the Rose Garden and the terraces below. On this level, we planted massive herbaceous borders, which I planted with blue and purple flowers. The

borders are very deep and long, so it was essential to use shrubs as a background, and herbaceous plants in unusually large clumps, with as many as twenty-five plants in a clump.

I was also asked to redesign the Rose Garden. This area is the principal design feature of the gardens at Eaton Hall. Because I consider rose gardens to require a certain formality, I designed a geometric parterre of hedged enclosures (evocative of Detmar Blow's 1911 plan of a neo-Elizabethan topiary garden for this area). The area consists of four separate rose gardens, each of a different colour and geometric pattern. We redesigned the trellised timber pillars used as climbing frames along each outer edge, topping them with trellis urns and adding another line of them to form walkways on each side of the outer balustrades; these pillars are joined by a thick rope on to which the roses are tied, providing height and definition and allowing framed views along the two far sides of the garden. Eight newly planted mature Irish yews on the outside of the four gardens add further height and maturity. We also redesigned Detmar Blow's central canal, which runs the length of the terrace and divides the Rose Garden. Two existing sculptures make terrific eye-catchers.

I designed each rose garden with four outer beds and a central bed with a topiary yew at the centre. In the outer beds I placed trellis pyramids on which climbing roses and clematis are planted, with a mixture of old-fashioned and floribunda roses and perpetual-flowering English roses. A few herbaceous plants provide colour continuity and interest later on in the season.

To the south of the house, the Dragon Fountain Garden and its parterre were in great need of restoration. The garden was thought to have been designed by Edwin Lutyens but, although there were no existing plans, I was convinced that it was Nesfield – early photographs of the garden resembled the designs of Nesfield's East Terraces and the materials used were typical of him. Photographs taken in the early 1900s showed that the present, rather angular geometric pattern of beds had originally been more pleasingly curved. I decided that a reinterpretation of the original design would be highly effective. Rather than using the planting that Nesfield would have used, we replanted, using a selection of bedding plants that were more three-dimensional and, ranging from dark burgundy to pale pink, gave the parterre more colour. Large box balls and yew pyramids of the Nesfield planting were replaced. The urns and statues were put back to their original positions and the fountain was restored, as were the other ornaments and fountains all over the garden. Finally, we removed many saplings which had grown over the years and obscured the wonderful view to the south into the larger landscape.

Below the top terrace is a long walk which leads to an area that needed attention. As it was shady I felt that this would be the ideal place for a woodland garden, which would be an interesting way of linking the rather formal main gardens with this end of the garden, where there was another huge herbaceous border, a vast kitchen garden and a beautiful camellia house. I kept the long, gravelled walk and designed large borders on either side, planting them with white-flowering plants, with clumps of *Rhododendron × mucronatum* and 'Dora Amateis' at intervals and, in front, clumps of white *Pulmonaria* 'Sissinghurst White' and double white primulas. This theme

repeats itself all the way down against a background of shrubs and a row of eight white *Prunus* 'Shirotae'. Beyond, the theme gets more informal and mown paths run through large borders and long grass. The large beds are planted with rhododendrons, daphnes and cornus, with auriculas and hellebores as groundcover. At the centre of these beds there is a circular grassy glade surrounded by a ring of magnolias and a stone seat placed in a direct line with another similar seat at the opposite end of the garden. The grass paths lead further along to a collection of hamamelis, more magnolias and the hot borders, which are planted with herbaceous plants and grasses in all shades of red, orange and russets to flower in late summer.

A tall brick wall backs the herbaceous border and separates the garden from the vegetable garden, which I redesigned. Further away, to the south, there is an Arts and Crafts Teahouse Garden and the Herb Garden, which needed replanting and its seats and gates redesigning – work that has just been completed.

While I was working on the gardens we restored many other features, such as the ha-ha; we also looked at all the hedges, general tree planting and opening up vistas. I also designed a master plan to improve the Deer Park, which the Duke is reinstating. Hundreds of trees are being planted. I designed two large avenues which radiate from the corners of the house. One is planted with ash; the other with horse chestnuts in clumps of eight, leading towards a huge mound of spoil, which I have redesigned to imitate a circular ring fort. At the centre there will be a taller flat mound with a labyrinth cut out of the grass.

Because the estate is so large, our work at Eaton Hall is substantial. From the start we drew up a fifteen-year plan and

programme for restoration, design and maintenance of the gardens and fabric – the water, walls, paths, terraces and statues. I am still working on new ideas: the large boggy sloping area between the third terrace and the lake presents a marvellous opportunity for a large water feature linking the canal from the upper terraces to the lake.

I found Eaton Hall unique: so interesting, with so much history to be acknowledged or reinterpreted, and so much scope for new ideas. There is an element of a jigsaw puzzle about it – finding out its past, and putting things like statues back where they originally belonged. There is terrific enthusiasm and skill in the head gardener and his staff, and a communal pride in the task. It was wonderful, too, to find in the Duke and Duchess two people who wanted to do all this work, who were interested in restoring every fountain, re-invigorating every hedge and mulching every tree. Our work at Eaton Hall continues to be a wonderful experience – from thinking about the colour of the ironwork to restoring the camellia house, Eaton Hall really is total involvement.

Above, left to right The top terrace projects like the prow of a ship into large herbaceous borders below the walls. A pink border on the side of the Dragon Fountain planted with pink lavender, *Penstemon* 'Hewitt's Pink' and *Eupatorium purpureum* backed by *Cotinus* 'Grace' and *Lavatera* 'Burgundy Wine'. A blue border on the same level as the Rose Garden, planted with delphiniums, *Campanula lactiflora, Phlox paniculata* 'Blue Paradise', *Thalictrum delavayi* 'Hewitt's Double' and *T. rochebruneanum*, veronicas and *Nepeta grandiflora* 'Bramdean', *Artemisia* and *Sedum* 'Herbstfreude' (Autumn Joy). In the woodland garden, grass paths winding past *Rhododendron augustinii*, magnolias and *Viburnum carlesii* with *Leucojum aestivum* rising next to *Daphne mezereum* and a clump of bergenias.

Above *Molinia caerulea* 'Moorhexe' and red *Monarda* 'Cambridge Scarlet'.
Left *Digitalis ferruginea*, *Geum* 'Mrs J. Bradshaw' and *Monarda* 'Cambridge Scarlet'.
Below left *Crocosmia* 'Lucifer'.
Below Design for the trelliswork urns which we designed to serve as finials on the trellised timber pillars in the Rose Garden.
Right A tall, red-bricked wall separates the kitchen garden from the hot borders. Different hues of red flowers mix well with grasses like *Miscanthus*, *Stipa gigantea* and *Molinia*. *Helenium* 'Rubinkuppel' and *Monarda* 'Squaw' are planted all the way along the long border.

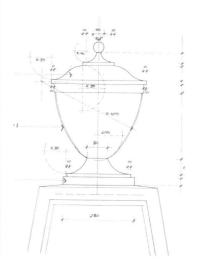

A FRENCH FAIRYTALE

Château de Reux

Château de Reux is a small moated castle, with a pretty dovecote tower, just outside Pont-l'Eveque in Normandy. It is situated near the bottom of a hill, with a garden that slopes down northwards. When I first saw the château there was no garden; the house was surrounded by stone paving – Versailles-style *pavé du roi*, which is attractive but here seemed too cold and severe. The walls of both the château and the moat were covered in ivy and, beyond the moat were the remnants of an overgrown, claustrophobic evergreen landscape planting, with Portugal laurel, box, yew and thuja trees. The atmosphere was gloomy, and the young owners wanted a garden with a softer, more open feeling.

First I took all the ivy down and the walls were restored. Then I designed the new gardens next to the house around two axes, running north–south and east–west. To the east of the north–south axis, the space is divided in two. Next to the house I left an area of the *pavé du roi* to make a small entrance courtyard; beside it is the little square dovecote garden, where a small area of lawn is surrounded with thickly planted borders.

The other end of the garden has a very irregular shape, so to achieve a balanced design I planted, at the western end of the east–west axis, four blocks of yew which radiate inwards from a curved hedge. At the four inner points of the yew are planted four *Malus tschonoskii*. This grouping creates a structural endpoint to the axis line. In this garden, outside the drawing room, the planting, intended to look its best in August, includes roses, phlox, asters and penstemons.

The pivot of the new garden is at the intersection of the axial paths, where I planted four *Prunus* ×

Above The château's head gardener, the invaluable M. Joseph Tasson.
Right *Rosa* 'New Dawn' spills over the walls of the moat and extends along the bridge to the garden on the other side. *Hydrangea anomala* subsp. *petiolaris*, clouds of *Pyrus salicifolia* and the domed dovecote tower create a fairytale atmosphere. Two clumps of *Phyllostachys nigra* are on the other side of the bridge.

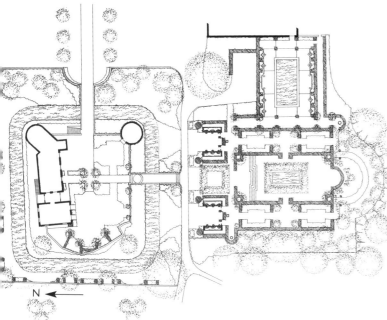

yedoensis. From here, a wide, central path runs north to the bridge and the gardens beyond the moat. On either side of the bridge there are two pyramids of *Rosa* 'Iceberg' and *Clematis* 'Henryi', with, behind them, two *Pyrus salicifolia* cropped in the shape of an umbrella.

For continuity, I planted *Rosa* 'New Dawn' on the walls all the way around the moat. The area close to the water is planted very simply with gunnera, alchemilla and viburnum. On the west and south side of the moat, borders with buttresses of yew give symmetry and rhythm.

To lighten and give depth to the garden on the other side of the moat, I carved out two small trellised garden rooms from the dense wall of evergreen shrubbery, and planted one in white, the other in yellow and mauve. Unfortunately, over the next few years the wind and age decimated the trellis's evergreen background, so we removed the thicket completely and extended the garden to its furthest extent. I was left with the two trellis rooms set in a large, open area which sloped downwards dramatically, so the gardens that were to fill in this area needed also to provide a backing for the trellis rooms.

The design consists of formal garden rooms and walks which rely on hedges and foliage for main effect and are thus relatively low-maintenance. Between the trellis rooms is a square lawn. From here a wide, shallow flight of grass steps, edged with white stone, leads to a long rectangular pool surrounded by pleached hornbeam. On either side of this space are a pair of wide, hedged yew walks, each with buttresses of yew forming three rooms – two large ones intersected by a smaller, transitional room. At the end there is a semicircular, scented walk planted with lilac, honeysuckle and philadelphus. To give the walk a unified theme, I planted each of the large rooms as a foliage garden: one with grey-green foliage plants, one with yellow, one with silver and one with purple. The two square transitional rooms are very simple, each with four *Acer pseudoplatanus* 'Brilliantissimum', one at each corner, and a central seat against the yew hedge. Entering this space you can look back along the simple lines of the design towards the lusher planting around the château, which rises like a castle in a fairytale.

Left, above A high pleached hedge of hornbeam gives a cloistered air to the peaceful green central pool garden.
Far left The garden plan; at the top left is a swimming-pool garden added later.
Left After crossing the bridge, a path made of *pave du roi* leads you past pyramids of *Rosa* 'Iceberg' to the pool and the gardens beyond.
Right, top to bottom The dovecote garden, planted with *Rosa* 'Penelope' and santolina; pyramids of *Rosa* 'Iceberg' with contrasting underplanting; looking back towards the château from one of the outer yew-framed garden enclosures, here the silver garden.

A CONTEMPORARY INTERPRETATION OF A VICTORIAN GARDEN

Ascott House

Built as a hunting box in the late nineteenth century by Leopold de Rothschild, Ascott is a long, low-built, black-and-white half-timbered house lying along a ridge with magnificent views over the surrounding Buckinghamshire countryside. The garden was completed in about 1900 with the help of the famous nurseryman Sir Harry Veitch, and was noted at the time for its horticultural excellence, in particular for the range and colour of the evergreens as well as for the elaborate topiary that was grown throughout the garden. Today, while the family still occupy and run the house and garden, it belongs to the National Trust, who were given it in 1949 by Anthony de Rothschild. Over the years the garden had suffered, like so many others of that period, and when about fifteen years ago I was asked to help, much of it was sadly down at heel.

Lady Victoria de Rothschild asked me to help improve the public gardens, to incorporate roses and herbaceous borders, and to create a private garden around the house. Because of the garden's illustrious history I decided to use the tradition of evergreen planting and topiary as the structural elements of a contemporary interpretation of a Victorian garden. I embarked on what was to be a long association with this garden, designing

Right Outside the library I designed a little knot of box and lavender, with a central post of clipped medlar. From here, I left an open view to the countryside, past great square blocks of yew.

Right, below In the black-and-white garden, zigzag hedges of clipped box decorate corner beds surrounding a central square bed containing a cruciform pattern of box. White roses and clematis are underplanted with 'Black Parrot' and 'Queen of Night' tulips, *Leucojum aestivum*, *Bergenia* 'Silberlicht', *Dianthus* 'Mrs Sinkins', *Anthriscus sylvestris* 'Ravenswing', *Cosmos atrosanguineus*, black double poppies and *Centaurea cyanus* 'Black Boy'. Along the edge the square blocks of the yew hedge contain *Prunus pissardii* 'Nigra'. In summer the arch to the right becomes a covered walk leading to the brown garden.

Below Topiary shapes now fill the Sunken Garden, where patterns of clipped box are enclosed and echoed by solid buttresses of yew hedging.

and improving different areas at different times. She was very involved with the design from the first; she had excellent taste and was quite daring in her ideas and very interested in colour combinations; it was fascinating and rewarding to work with her.

Because the house is so long and narrow, I designed the private gardens around it as a series of separate garden spaces, giving each a different character. To make the enclosure of the gardens more interesting, the divisions are marked by wooden fencing that I designed and had painted black to echo the black timbers of the house; the fencing supports espaliered apples. The whole is given unity by long hedges of yew on the outer, south side. Along this, at the beginning and end of each garden room, the yew is grown out in the shape of a square block, inside which I planted a standard *Prunus pissardii* 'Nigra', the dark-leaved prunus, which is clipped in the shape of a ball. These elegant vertical elements form decorative punctuation points, breaking the almost uninterrupted line of hedge and adding a certain formality and rhythm. The leaves are a dark burgundy, which is, for me, a very Victorian colour.

At the head of the gardens on the eastern side of the house is a pretty herb garden, designed within the existing walls of what had been an L-shaped service court. The garden is paved and divided into three squares. The first, which you see as you enter, has blocks of box at each corner, with various creeping thymes covering the rest of the space and surrounding a handsome terracotta pot. The other two are planted with mint, thyme, camomile, chives, parsley, tarragon and origanum, with *Iris* 'Florentina' at the corners to give structure. At the intersection of the paths, there are three metal pergolas planted with *Rosa* 'The Garland' and various white-flowering clematis such as *Clematis armandii*, *C.* 'White Moth' and *C.* 'Jackmanii Alba'. The surrounding borders are filled with roses underplanted with violas, lavender and flowering herbs. There are espaliered apples and pears along the walls, and on the south and north sides yew hedges form two alcoves, each holding a seat and lovely terracotta jars.

From the herb garden, steps lead down to a wooden pergola clothed with wisteria, and on into the spring garden – a walk with very wide borders planted with early-flowering bulbs: narcissi and tulips in white and yellow, and white-flowering

Clockwise from top left The plan for the Sunken Garden; the overall design of the garden; an unrealized plan for a labyrinth – I did, however, create the serpentine walk which links the area at the front of the house to the lily pond. The planting on the main terrace includes *Nepeta* 'Six Hills Giant', roses 'Empress Josephine', 'Souvenir de la Malmaison', 'William Lobb', 'Baronne Adolph de Rothschild' and 'Cardinal de Richelieu', *Campanula lactiflora* and *C. l.* 'Loddon Anna'.

plants such as *Dicentra spectabilis* 'Alba', white primulas and iris, *Pulmonaria* 'Sissinghurst White' and *Euphorbia amygdaloides* var. *robbiae*. At the centre of the borders on both sides I planted the wonderfully architectural *Cornus controversa* 'Variegata', whose branches spread in layers, and at the entrance a hedge of *Sarcococca humilis*; these together with choysia, clipped box and, at the back of the border, *Viburnum tinus* give structure to the planting. The garden is almost all white – the yellow tulips appeared by mistake, but they add the right touch – and the effect is ethereal and fresh.

The spring walk leads on to the dining-room terrace, which is very simple – square and paved with a basketweave pattern of small Dutch bricks. The criss-crossing lines of bricks, with the areas in between inlaid with small stones and moss colonizing the spaces, have a very pretty and decorative effect, making the terrace a pleasant place for the family to eat in the summer, all enclosed by a yew hedge. Sculpted box surrounds narrow borders planted with standard *Viburnum carlesii* at the corners, and standard *Rosa xanthina* 'Canary Bird' on either side of the French windows. Through a narrow archway a small corridor opens out into the main south border gardens in front of the drawing room. The terrace is wide with an open view between the beds opposite the house, and the surrounding borders are planted so that there is something in flower all year round. A mainly pink colour scheme is backed by topiary, planted for structure and also as a dominant feature: both in beds and pots, box is grown and clipped in a ziggurat effect. Big clumps of

Left, top to bottom Box topiary in pots and beds on the main terrace; the view from the main terrace through the rose garden, whose beds are edged with box squares, santolina and borders of *Nepeta* 'Six Hills Giant', to a pillar of *Rosa* 'Climbing Iceberg' – the central feature of the black-and-white garden; planting in the brown garden includes berberis, *Pittosporum tenuifolium* 'Tom Thumb', *Tulipa* 'Rococo', *Euphorbia dulcis* 'Chameleon', *Salvia officinalis* 'Purpurascens' and *Epimedium* x *warleyense*.
Right A handsome urn acts as a centrepiece to one of three square beds in the herb garden. Blocks of box mark each corner and the bed is filled with a tapestry carpet of creeping thymes.
Below My design for a seat for the South Borders.

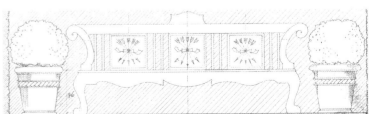

Rosa 'Felicia' underplanted with clumps of strawberries and violas are surrounded by *Lavandula angustifolia* 'Loddon Pink' and *L. a.* 'Munstead', pink helianthemums, geraniums, artemisia, pink Japanese anemones, purple salvias and *Rosa* 'Gruss an Aachen'. The walls of the house are planted with climbing roses 'Noisette Carnée', 'Gloire de Dijon' and 'Climbing Souvenir de la Malmaison', ceanothus, *Clematis* 'Victoria' and *C.* 'Maidwell Hall' and *Wisteria sinensis*.

At the end of the drawing-room terrace, the path becomes very narrow between wide borders edged with *Nepeta* 'Six Hills Giant'. These are filled with old-fashioned shrub roses, including 'Souvenir de la Malmaison', 'Baronne Adolph de Rothschild', 'Fantin-Latour', 'Cardinal de Richelieu', 'Empress Josephine', 'Tour de Malakoff', 'William Lobb' and 'Ispahan'.

At the front of the borders, at each corner, are big platforms of box shaped as interlocking squares, which serve to anchor the exuberant planting.

A path serving as an opening to the wider landscape separates the romantic informality of the rose garden from the intricate geometry of the black-and-white garden. Here all the woodwork is painted black and the flowers are a combination of white and dark burgundy. The central bed – a square, set diagonally within the overall square shape of this garden – contains a cross outlined in box. *Rosa* 'Yvonne Rabier' grows within each arm; in the centre a frame supports *R.* 'Climbing Iceberg' and *Clematis alipina* subsp. *sibirica* 'White Moth'. Surrounding this bed are four triangular corner beds with a stepped pattern of box, echoing the zigzag shape of the central bed, containing large

Left To give structure and rhythm to the Madeira Walk and to break up the long lines of planting, I divided the borders into sections, repeated planting groups and placed urns planted with a purple *Cordyline australis* at regular intervals. In early summer, the soft mauves, purples and pinks of *Rosa* 'William Lobb', *Delphinium* 'Conspicuous' and *D.* 'Turkish Delight', *Salvia* x *sylvestris* 'Mainacht', *Nepeta grandiflora* 'Bramdean' and *N. racemosa* 'Walker's Low' glow against the backdrop of a golden yew hedge and a wall overhung with holly.

Above, top The Madeira Walk was planted to look good right up until autumn, when the colours deepen. Here, late-flowering *Aster* x *frikartii* 'Mönch', *Penstemon* 'Alice Hindley' and *P. f.* 'Port Wine' amongst others, and rich clumps of *Sedum* 'Herbstfreude' (Autumn Joy) come into their own. It is a good example of rhythm in a border.

Above White tulips and narcissi, with a sprinkling of yellow tulips, shine brightly in the spring borders. *Cornus controversa* 'Variegata' spreads its horizontal tiers to architectural effect – there is one on either side, so they are the dominant feature in the border – while clipped box topiary adds further structural interest.

Above and below | I designed the kitchen garden in a neglected area near the swimming-pool gardens. The box-edged beds are filled with vegetables, fruit, herbs and cut flowers for the house. The paths are made of hoggin, which is very practical in this sort of garden. Some beds are edged with step-over apples. I designed decorative gazebos for soft fruit to go at the centre of the four main square beds, and the pretty pale blue seats placed under vine-covered archways.

clumps of *Rosa* 'Iceberg' and, in the outer corners, four standard *R.* 'Yvonne Rabier'. The underplanting combines white leucojum with tulips and herbaceous plants in black and deep burgundy.

The last garden on the south side fulfilled the client's unusual and, for me, challenging request for a brown garden. In contrast to the previous complex patterns, the layout is simply formal, with two rectangular beds indented to make a hexagonal central space, which seems to emerge from two covered walks at either end – tunnels over which grow the browny-purple-leaved *Vitis vinifera* 'Purpurea' and the deep red *Rosa* 'Guinée' with *Lonicera* × *americana*. The beds are surrounded by a copper beech hedge and have matched planting: in the centre of each is *R.* 'Julia's Rose' (parchment copper shades) with two acers either side; behind, filling each corner, are *Cotinus coggygria* 'Royal Purple' and *Sambucus nigra* 'Guincho Purple'. The rest of the border is planted with clumps of *Salvia officinalis* 'Purpurascens', *Verbascum* 'Helen Johnson', *Digitalis parviflora*, *Plantago major* 'Rubrifolia' and, in front, *Heuchera mircrantha* var. *diversifolia* 'Palace Purple', *Trifolium repens* 'Purpurascens' and *Viola* 'Molly Sanderson'. Next to the acers are clumps of *Rosa* 'The Prince'. The underplanting

includes dark hellebores, *Anthriscus sylvestris* and *Foeniculum vulgare* 'Purpureum'. *Iris* 'Brown Chocolate' and *I.* 'Kent Pride' are planted along the covered walks and next to the heuchera.

At the end of the terrace, the view is closed by a semicircular yew hedge with a large seat which I designed. The garden wraps round the house with great topiary squares of yew, leading past a little early summer garden and ending in the Library Garden, where I designed a small knot of box and lavender.

I planned the gardens – which are known collectively as the South Borders – to complement the architecture of the house, with each garden having a different character and relating to a particular part. There is a change in atmosphere and pace, as geometrically shaped garden rooms give way to softer-edged walks with wide borders. In addition to the open view from the main terrace, the long line of the enclosing yew hedge is broken at two further points to open up the view from the house to the countryside beyond. One vista, between the south border and the black-and-white garden, is lined with espaliered apples and white irises; the other, between the black-and-white garden and the brown garden, has dark-toned heuchera.

My next project was the Sunken Garden, once a fern garden, which had fallen into disrepair. Because of the rectangular shape of the area and because it could be viewed from above, the obvious solution to me was a topiary pattern, so I surrounded the garden with a yew hedge which encloses a design of square and circular box hedges linked with gravel paths – a modern, three-dimensional interpretation of a parterre, using simple shapes. In the centre is a fountain with a seat on either side with *Acer pseudoplatanus* 'Brilliantissimum' planted for spring colour. For the centre of the four patterns I designed tall urns on plinths made of open ironwork and these are covered with a small-leaved ivy.

At the base of a path leading down a slope was a rather dull grass mound, which I planted with spiralling yew hedges. This not only transformed the mound but also led you down towards the next garden at a lower level, the Madeira Walk. This long walk, another part of the historical garden, is very narrow, with borders only 2 metres (7 feet) wide – which made them difficult to plant, particularly since on one side there is a wall with a holly hedge above it, and on the other a golden yew hedge. The border was to be planted with herbaceous plants in shades of blue, mauve and dusky pink and, because it was in the public area, it was important that there was something to look at from spring to autumn. I decided to divide it into nine sections and to repeat elements in order to give it structure and rhythm. In alternate bays I either planted a large clump of *Cynara cardunculus* (Scolymus Group)

'Violetto di Chioggia' or placed a grey urn on a plinth – planted with tulips in the spring and dark burgundy cordyline in the summer. In front of these I planted *Sedum* 'Herbstfreude', and behind them, *Galega orientalis*. At the beginning, end and in the centre of this very long border, I planted clumps of *Rosa* 'Reine des Violettes' 'Souvenir du Docteur Jamain', 'Tuscany Superb' and *R.* × *odorata* 'Pallida'. Other herbaceous plants in the border include *Nepeta grandiflora* 'Bramdean', *Symphytum* × *uplandicum*, *Phlox paniculata* 'Lilac Time', *Delphinium* 'Turkish Delight', *Campanula lactiflora* 'Loddon Anna', *Delphinium* 'Strawberry Fair', *Lupinus missouriensis*, *Aster* × *frikartii*, alliums, salvias and violas.

Above *Delphinium* 'Turkish Delight'

In another historical area, the Venus fountain, we designed two astrological topiary gardens – one to reflect the position of the planets at my client's birth, the other the planets at her husband's, calculated by an astrologer. Metal topiary shapes of each planet were planted in yew and holly; the moon was planted in white variegated holly and the sun in variegated golden yew. To give the area a homogeneous shape we added some simple cones of yew underplanted with ivy and thyme to form two concentric circles. (This garden has recently been changed.)

I was also asked to redesign the garden round an existing tennis court and create a new vegetable garden. The bones of the vegetable garden, the walls and hedges, were there, but the garden had been abandoned. I designed it with hoggin paths and beds edged in step-over apples, and added four gazebos for soft fruit.

During the years I worked at Ascott, I was involved in almost every aspect of the garden. I planted walks, and made a wild garden in a corner that had been neglected, a new entrance drive and a scented walk. We reorganized the greenhouses, made and relaid paths, remade steps, improved lawns, planted bulbs. I was asked to design a labyrinth but sadly that was not planted, though I did create a serpentine walk. I loved this garden passionately and it became part of my life – which was wrong because it wasn't my garden, although I felt as though it was. I enjoyed it because it was so challenging, and it was hard to detach myself, as I had been deeply connected to it and I took it all very personally. Quite like a love affair, really.

CONTRASTS AND CONNECTIONS

Thorpe Hall

Thorpe Hall in Suffolk is a charming pink brick Jacobean house surrounded by a moat. In 1988 I was asked to redesign the garden round the house and to create a small park from the field on the other side of the moat.

I started with the entrance courtyard. Because of the period of the house, I felt that it needed a structured, formal entrance, so I planted a box parterre that was modern in design, clipping the box into block-like, flat shapes, with two central pyramids of yew for height. The whole parterre is backed by a beech hedge.

Around the house there were other beech hedges, which I moved and added to so as to divide the existing garden into new, smaller areas. To the east of the house I designed three seasonal garden rooms, each with a simple theme. In the south-east corner I made a small garden with four L-shaped corner beds of late-summer-flowering herbaceous plants in tones of purple and blue. Beech hedges divide this area from the next one, which is a small winter garden. Here I wanted deciduous trees whose skeletons

Above The bee orchid, native to this area, has naturalized in the meadows.
Left The four Irish yews are an important vertical element in this luscious rose garden. Water is not only pleasing because of its sound; it also enhances the smell of the roses.
Below, left to right The pool is surrounded by beds of Hybrid Musk roses 'Prosperity' and 'Moonlight'; entrances should always be simple – here plain clipped platforms are combined with pyramids and hedges; the contrast of long and short grass and the close-mown mound, like a sculpture in the centre of a copper beech circle; the plan of the garden.

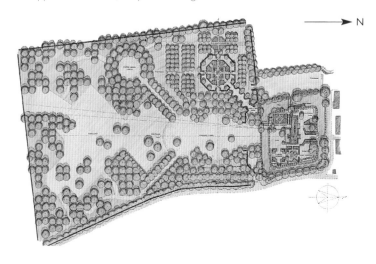

would glow in winter light, so I planted a small grove of multi-stemmed *Betula utilis* var. *jacquemontii* (the white-barked birch) with a sheet of *Crocus tommasinianus* beneath. The third area is an early summer garden, simply planted with various lilacs and *Philadelphus* 'Belle Etoile'. Mown paths wind through this area and lead to a seat backed by hollies and *Osmanthus × burkwoodii*.

On the south side of the house, outside the kitchen, I designed a formal herb garden. Brick-paved and lined with hedges of Rosa Mundi, it has four triangular herb beds edged with box decorated with topiary cones and balls. The triangles surround a square of clipped box comprising nine small square compartments for herbs.

Between the herb garden and the late summer garden, there is a lawn sprinkled with apple trees. Across from the lawn, on the other side of the moat, was the field where the owners wanted to plant a park. As this was to be the main vista, it had to look interesting when viewed from the house. I like the idea of opening and closing views, screening off some and opening up others, allowing one to see specific eye-catchers, so I planted trees in patterns that move in and out. I broke up the expanse

into different areas and walks that become apparent only as you move through the park. To the south-west, for example, I planted a circle of copper beech, surrounding a grass mound which my clients built out of the spoil from digging out the swimming pool. This is reached by a walk of alternate ash and beech. I planted oaks all the way along the boundary between the field and the road, and interplanted them with may trees, white-flowering and pink-flowering ones placed alternately. From the house there are views to the end of the parkland, with lines and curves of trees enclosing areas each side. It was great fun being able to plant a park. I planted mostly parkland trees like oak and beech; although I brought in some mature trees to give some height to the planting, most of the new trees were planted as whips and will grow the better for this.

To make a connection between the gardens on the near side of the moat and the area immediately beyond, and also to anchor the rose garden I was making in the west side of the field, I designed a serpentine hornbeam walk. It begins immediately beyond the moat and leads right into the rose garden, so the

hedges link the garden back to the house as well as bringing the garden into the field.

The rose garden itself is octagonal; an outer octagon of yew and an inner octagon of wooden trellis create an enclosed grass walk around the garden. You enter the garden by the hornbeam walk, or through one of four openings in the yew hedge, under arches, covered with climbing roses, that link the yew to the trellis. Cypresses are planted at the four corners of each arch and on the corners of the inner beds, providing structural punctuation points and vertical contrast with the rounded form of the roses.

Within the rose garden, paths paved with a local red brick divide the area into eight beds, at each corner of the octagon, that are planted with old-fashioned roses. In the centre is a pool and fountain with channels leading to four smaller triangular pools like arrows. Around these are four corner-shaped beds planted with Hybrid Musk roses which form a broken square around the pool. The narrow channels make the brick path appear to float over the water. The planting is orchestrated to make a voluptuous display in high summer: the outer borders, heavy with the heady perfume of old roses, are mostly pink and purple-red, while the inner ones are glowing white, with the Hybrid Musks promising a repeat flowering later in the season.

Beyond, there is a kitchen garden, also octagonal. An orchard with mown paths cut through long grass surrounds the two. I love the contrasts and connections at Thorpe, between the contained garden around the house and the expansive area beyond the moat, between the parkland and the formally planted areas.

Above left Old-fashioned roses *Rosa* 'Duc de Guise', 'Duchesse de Montebello', 'Henri Martin' and 'Robert le Diable' in the rose garden.
Above *Rosa nutkana* 'Plena', *R.* 'Prosperity' and *R.* 'Felicia' with *Salvia × sylvestris* 'Mainacht' beneath them.
Pages 168–9 In the small herb garden, hedged with Rosa Mundi, topiary shapes contrast with the flowing, lax form of the surrounding clumps of *Rosa* 'Felicia' and the sword-shaped leaves of *Iris* 'Florentina'.

A GARDEN ON MANY LEVELS

A Garden in Spain

Just above the Mediterranean, near Marbella, is a low-built, modern house whose gardens extend over what were once three separate plots – the original, on which the house stands, and a further two which were acquired a few years later. My task was to connect the three plots and make them into one cohesive, harmonious garden. However, the later additions were at a much lower level, separated from the house by a high wall on one side and a ravine 20 metres (70 feet) deep on the other. Because the ravine served as a drainage conduit to the sea from the hills above, it could not be filled in; so, in order to unite the pieces of land, engineers had first to encase the gully in a concrete shell, and fill the resulting depression with soil.

This still left a site with major differences of level, and we had to make a design that would flow naturally from one separate area to another, and that would use awkward changes in level to aesthetic advantage. The essence of my design was to terrace the site; to use water both as a unifying link between the separate areas and to exploit the changes in level for dramatic effect; and to use traditional Spanish style – and a contemporary interpretation of it – to add a sense of harmony to the whole.

Right Water, in pools, rills and fountains, is the dominant motif in this garden, linking different parts of the garden and, as in this water staircase, using the many distinct levels to create drama and movement.

Far right, top to bottom White *Nerium oleander*; a paving design; *Thunbergia grandiflora*; a design for a finial for a pavilion; *Brugmansia arborea* 'Knightii'.

Below A statue of a horse, sculpted by Belinda Eade, rears up from a grotto and waterfall set into a high retaining wall separating the original garden from the lower level of the new.

The house and its original garden, with a lawn divided by a kidney-shaped pool, are on the uppermost level. To the south and east of this are the new gardens, all at a lower level. The garden begins with a courtyard (originally planned as an entrance courtyard but not used as such), which is surrounded by pleached large-leaved *Ficus rubiginosa*, with a hedge of the small-leaved *F. benjamina* below; beneath the figs I planted a drift of yellow clivia, which shines against the green. In the centre of the courtyard is a two-tiered fountain, the first of the succession of descending fountains that help unify this garden. This one is surrounded by four cypresses, with *Rosa* 'Maréchal Niel' growing through them.

Left The water steps, lined with *Brugmansia arborea* 'Knightii' and *Aeonium arboreum* 'Zwartkop', link the orange tree garden with the pool garden below. Water flows from the bowl on a pedestal at the top of the steps down to a sunken pool.
Right The garden plan.
Below A charming wooden seat painted blue is set below the walls surrounding the orange tree garden; it looks across an antique fountain set in a pretty small terrace to the pergola planted with *Thunbergia grandiflora*.

Left A cypress hedge encloses the orange tree garden where clipped myrtle edges formal, symmetrical beds surrounding a beautiful terrace, decorated with traditional patterns of pebbles. The beds are planted with orange and lemon trees and other white-flowerd plants with some touches of blue planting, including agapanthus and *Felicia amelloides*.

Top right Water on the highest level of the garden is provided by an elegant two-tier fountain in the entrance courtyard. It is set in a simple octagonal bed framed by four cypresses and surrounded by a hedge of *Ficus benjamina*, topped with tall pleached *F. rubiginosa*.

Middle right Another blue-painted seat looks under the long arm of the L-shaped pergola that surrounds the pool garden. It sits on a small, sunny terrace halfway down the flight of steps that leads from the original garden on the upper level to the wide sloping lawn below the pergola.

Below right The Moorish inspiration in the pool garden is evident in the *mirador*-like pavilion and the jets of water, like those found at the Alhambra, arching across the dark pool. But the design is given a contemporary interpretation, with the cool green lawn intersected by long thin lines of white stone, marking a geometric grid.

Three steps lead down from the simplicity of this space to the orange tree garden, which is both architectural and graceful, with a fountain at either end, in the shape of shallow bowls on pedestals. The terrace is paved with patterns of pebbles in the traditional manner, the work of a Seville family who have specialized for generations in this type of paving. A father and son team did the terrace here. This garden is surrounded by a tall cypress hedge and the borders, which are edged with box, are planted with orange and lemon trees and white and blue flowers – white *Rosa* 'Iceberg' in groups, underplanted with *Felicia amelloides*. At the corners of the borders there are small clumps of *Crinum × powellii* 'Album', and in the central beds more 'Iceberg', this time combined with *Agapanthus africanus* 'Albus'. Jasmine is planted near the steps, and on a summer's evening the scent is intoxicating.

From this terrace, a water staircase of fourteen steps elegantly signals a change in level; the water ripples down a narrow rill in the centre of the staircase to a small square

Above As elsewhere in the garden, fastigiate cypresses are used to provide vertical interest and punctuation points at the edge of separate garden areas. Here they mark the edge of the pool garden, contrasting with its curved jets of water and its horizontal lines of lawn and pool edging, and surrounded by echiums, the bold leaves of frangipani and the white blossoms of oleander.

sunken pool. At the top and lining the water staircase are white *Brugmansia arborea* 'Knightii' underplanted with *Aeonium arboreum* 'Zwartkop'. Parallel to the steps and emphasizing their elegant form, six olive trees are planted on the slope, with white olearia and white *Lagerstroemia indica*, underplanted with *Erigeron karvinskianus* and lavender.

Spreading around the orange tree courtyard are wide borders which follow the steps and, on the east side, sweep round the walls below the courtyard towards the tennis court; these are thickly planted with predominantly yellow and blue plants, with touches of pale buff, orange and white; they include *Brugmansia × candida* 'Grand Marnier', *Plectranthus grandiflora*, white bougainvillea, *Solanum rantonnetii*, *Cestrum nocturnum*, *Agapanthus africanus*, *Anisodontea thalictroides*, *Acacia pravissima*, *Vitex agnus-castus*, artemisia and a bold clump of *Beschorneria yuccoides*. Plumbago provides groundcover. The tennis court area is hidden down a few steps, and the court is sunken in order to conceal it further. A large, straw-roofed pavilion, designed by a local architect, and imported huge palm trees planted in exuberant borders also help to screen the court.

At the base of the water staircase, I designed a dramatic rectangular blue-black pool, with Alhambra-like jets arching from the sides. At the western end, a high wall separates this terrace from the original garden at the higher level, and here I made a waterfall, where the water gently cascades over a stone grotto from which the statue of a rearing horse emerges; the horse was sculpted from a single piece of rock by artist Belinda Eade, who also built the grotto. At right angles to this is an open pavilion raised on columns. This *mirador* is on the same level as the upper garden; here you can overlook the whole garden and gaze beyond to the mountains and the sea. Surrounding the pool and adding to the cool, contemporary feel is a lawn intersected with a geometric design of small strips of white stone.

To the east of the pool, another small, antique fountain is surrounded by more attractively patterned paving in the Spanish style. A seat faces a path which leads to the guest house under a wooden pergola; this pergola, covered with *Thunbergia grandiflora* and jasmine, encloses the lawn immediately around the pool.

On the far side of the long arm of the pergola is a large border which is planted with olive trees, *Rosa* 'Lovely Fairy', *Lavandula dentata* and *Osteospermum jucundum* 'Burgundy', with *Rosa* × *odoratum* 'Mutabilis' planted at regular intervals. Beyond is an expanse of sloping lawn, surrounded by olive trees, a grouping of pine trees and other boundary planting that edges the garden and screens a utility area.

Using trees typical of the Mediterranean merged the planting at the edge of the garden with the vegetation beyond in a natural way. In some places we used very large trees, specially imported to screen the garden along the boundary from the neighbouring properties. I did not want blocks of one colour and I wanted to mix different foliages. I planted *Cinnamomum camphora*, which is evergreen and a good shape, with leaves that are a very pale, glossy green when new, turning darker with age; it is quite fast-growing and it contrasts well with clumps of *Magnolia grandiflora*. I interspersed this with groups of three or five cypresses, which are a dominant feature throughout the garden, defining spaces and adding variety to a boundary planting. I broke up the monotony of the evergreens with groups of *Acca sellowiana*, a large grey-leaved plant with edible fruits, white hibiscus, white oleanders and *Pittosporum tenuifolium* 'Silver Queen', which has a variegated leaf. Where I had more space in front of the evergreens, I planted *Catalpa bignonioides* and *Melia azedarach*.

In a hot country it is very pleasant to entertain in the cool of the dark, so lighting was important, adding another dimension by allowing the garden to be seen in a completely different way. Lighting specialists helped design an effective and subtle scheme, using fibre optics. Some of the lighting on the trees is warm and some is cool, so that there are discreet differences throughout the garden. Minute, almost imperceptible lights show each step as well as each fountain; all the water features are subtly lit so that you are led from one area to another by the shape and movement of water.

Water is important at Casa Tania not only because it is cooling but also because it seamlessly unites the many different levels of the garden, running the length of the site through a series of fountains and rills. Just as I used the water to soothe and cool, so I designed the planting schemes to be lace-like and delicate, with soft colours – predominantly white, yellow and pink with some blue, lilac and grey. Because the area was so large, I wanted the garden to give a subtle impression. There are almost no bright colours – it is like a grey-green olive grove, with groups of black-green cypress planted in strategic places.

GARDENS AND WATERMEADOWS TRANSFORMED
Stanbridge Mill

Stanbridge Mill Farm stands on the River Allen in Dorset, one of England's best and most beautiful chalk streams, and the property includes several acres of ancient watermeadows. In 1992 the new owner asked me to redesign the areas close to the house to make an attractive garden, and improve and manage the neglected surrounding landscape. Owing to the ecological importance of the river and its watermeadows, the estate was declared a Site of Nature Conservation Interest, making this project even more interesting and challenging.

We prepared a management plan for the whole estate, which incorporated two specialist reports – one on the river, the other, by a consultant ecologist, on the watermeadows. Based on this we instigated a programme of replanting, cutting and laying hedges, restoring all fencing and planting clumps of trees and small woodlands particularly on the edges of the land, to enclose it while maintaining views across the countryside.

The existing garden was, I felt, rather suburban, and there was nowhere to sit. The area surrounding the house had not been dealt with well: the south front – potentially the prettiest side – was a tarmacked car park giving on to an intrusive and dangerous drive built to follow the shortest line from the main road to the Mill house. My first task was to re-route the drive to wind down a gentle slope to a new parking area to the south-east of the house. This meant that we could make a pretty paved sitting area and garden on the south side. This is separated from the car park by a yew hedge and is divided into two: a terrace paved in stone and brick and surrounded by beds leads into the summer garden, an expanse of lawn enclosed by borders planted with *Rosa* 'Penelope', *R.* 'Cornelia', ceanothus, *Phlomis samia*, *Geranium* 'Johnson's Blue' and *Hebe albicans*, edged with clipped box. Gaps in the borders allow lovely views through the parkland to a circular grove of birch trees, created by replanting together all the solitary birch trees we found scattered around the property. It is surrounded by a circular double beech hedge, which gives it a feeling of peace and seclusion.

From the south terrace a narrow walk edged with *Nepeta racemosa* 'Walker's Low' leads west to a smaller seating area

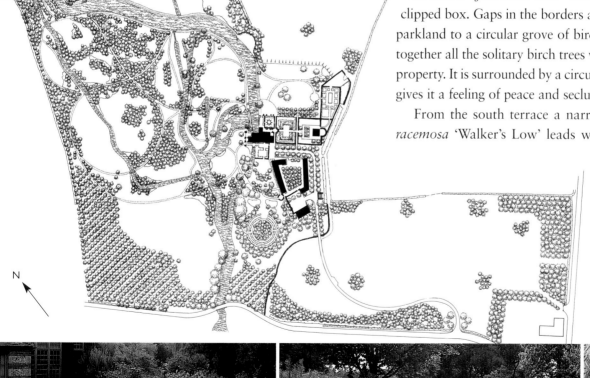

N

Far left *Cortaderia richardii* frames the house, which overlooks the River Allen. **Left** The plan of the garden. **Below, left to right** The garden outside the breakfast room, a green space surrounded by *Campanula lactiflora*, *Geranium* 'Johnson's Blue' and *Centranthus ruber*; a circle of yew hedges at an intersection of paths patterned with flint, tiles and brick; *Miscanthus sinensis* 'Malepartus'.

Top In the new garden to the south, a smooth green expanse of lawn slopes down to the river on the western side and a simple bridge crosses it lower down. Solid squares of box give weight to the planting where the lawn meets the terrace.

Above On the south terrace, standard roses are set inside box containers among catmint *Nepeta racemosa* 'Walker's Low' which will flower throughout the summer.

Right On the north side of the house, a new terrace is paved with basket-weave brick with a pattern of local knapped (split) flint. As flint is uncomfortable to walk on I used it only in small quantities, to add variety. Behind the terrace is a mound that evokes the prehistoric earthworks found in that part of Dorset and has the feel of a contemporary earth sculpture. Beyond, a double yew hedge, a beech hedge rising above it and then a double row of pleached limes create an intricate architectural vista. In front of the mound are beds of *Iris* 'Kent Pride', *Geranium* 'Johnson's Blue', *Stachys byzantina* and *Berberis thunbergii* f. *atropurpurea*.

overlooking the River Allen, where there are more mixed borders. The path leads round the house back to the river, where a bridge crosses the mill race to the gardens behind the house. Here there was originally a raised lawn and a low retaining wall had been built, which gave one the feeling of being in a ditch. I had to dig out that area to give myself a wide enough area to garden. In this space I created a series of gardens. The first, leading out from the breakfast room, is a simple lawn surrounded by borders next to the river. Then there is a prettily paved area where the owners can sit out: throughout the garden we took great care with the designs of paving patterns and incorporated local flint, brick and even roofing tiles. By the terrace I built a grass mound inspired by the many prehistoric burial mounds found in that part of Dorset. Standing about 3–4 metres (10–13 feet) high, it is surrounded by a low box hedge with a gravel path which spirals to the top of the mound.

Beyond that, on the east side of the house, a double yew hedge lines and hides a wide path, which is the main axis from the car park at the front to the back of the house, and divides the lower gardens and the gardens to the east. At an intersection of the path, wide steps lead up to a simple garden enclosed by cob walls on three sides, with a beech hedge to the west. Narrow borders contain red roses, *Chaenomeles* × *superba* 'Rowallane', crimson peonies and dark hellebores, all glowing red against the bright white walls. In the centre I planted a double rectangle of pleached limes, giving the garden the atmosphere of a cloister.

A door in the wall leads to the swimming-pool garden, under a black-painted pergola which runs the length of the wall. Planted on the arches are white roses such as 'Sander's White Rambler' and 'Climbing Iceberg' and white *Clematis* 'Henryi' and 'Marie Boisselot', underplanted with *Dianthus* 'Mrs Sinkins' and *Iris* 'White City'. The swimming-pool area is elegant and simple, with a pretty pavilion designed by John Stefanidis, surrounded by *Rosmarinus officinalis*, *Lavandula spica* 'Alba' and *Dianthus* 'Mrs Sinkins'. Clipped yew hedges surround the garden and form architectural features – for example, on one side of the pavilion buttresses of yew frame tall seats – and the whole area is surrounded by a yew hedge. On the pavilion side, a scented walk leads to the beech-hedged vegetable garden, where beds are laid out in a formal pattern.

The view of this whole area as you cross the bridge is fascinating. The different hedges form an intriguing and dynamic juxtaposition of colour and texture. The north side of the garden overlooks fields and a magnificent vista with a distant tower; in order to have an open view, I constructed a ha-ha by cutting into the existing chalk and facing it with metal netting. Now colonized with wildflowers, it looks natural and lovely. Along the garden side of the river, I planted huge clumps of *Iris sibirica* to make a decorative but natural-looking transition between the manicured garden and the watermeadows on the other side of the river.

We cleared the waterways, rebuilt dams and bridges and restored the watermeadows, removing the fallen and rotting vegetation. The meadow grass is now cut twice a year and this encourages the growth of wildflowers, which in turn brings wildlife. We also added new bridges in rustic style. At the furthest end of the watermeadows I designed a raised wooden walk which leads through a wet area to another delightful pavilion, also designed by John Stefanidis. Around this I planted varieties of miscanthus, shrubby willows like *Salix elaeagnos* subsp. *angustifolia* and *S. hookeriana*, and the native flag iris.

The watermeadow area had been badly planted in the 1970s, using species that were ill suited to very damp ground, and planting them in rigid tramlines. The natural mixed tree cover for wetland areas such as these includes three native species, willow, poplar and alder, so we reintroduced these trees in different ways. I planned a series of close-mown grass paths through the trees.

Stanbridge, with its combination of cultivated gardens and natural water, flora and fauna is unique. By unshackling the grounds and watermeadows from the constraints of years of neglect and bad planning, we were able to return the whole area to its natural beauty and magic.

Right, clockwise from top left Mown grass paths to a stone table in a glade; *Betula utilis* var. *jacquemontii*; a sculpture of a deer in the woodland; the terrace and breakfast-room garden; the pavilion at the far end of the property – ideal for birdwatching – engulfed in miscanthus and other grasses.
Below A plan of a paving feature in flint, tiles and brick.

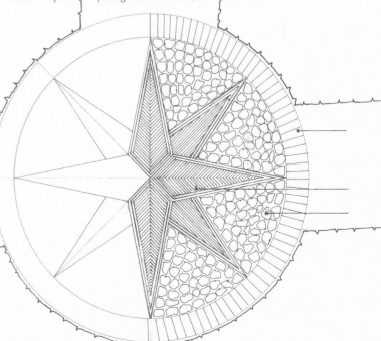

ELEGANT SIMPLICITY

La Bandiera

La Bandiera is a farmhouse in the hills of the Maremma, built on a hill with a view to the sea, with woodland above it – part of this is a nature reserve – as well as olive groves and vineyards on the sides and below. The surrounding landscape is beautiful, and there is no other house to be seen. This had always been a very simple farmhouse with no garden, and so I had a clean

canvas. My aim was to create a garden for my client, Lodovico Antinori, that was not only pretty but also did not compete with the views, and that was quite easy to maintain.

Lodovico Antinori didn't want to clutter the garden with cars, so he decided to build an underground garage, reached at one side down a steep ramp with high walls. He also built two new wings, on either side of the house, one for guests and the other for staff; with the house, these two additions formed an entrance courtyard which, because it was above the new garage, had a soil depth of only about 50 centimetres (20 inches).

My solution to the problem of shallow soil was to partially pave the courtyard. I designed a geometric pattern made up of paths constructed with blocks of tufa, combined with broad, flat rectangles of box and lavender, both of which thrive in these conditions. The tufa blocks were specially imported from Sicily because my client particularly liked the colour; tufa is a good paving material, as its porous nature means that it is easily colonized by moss and lichen, which quickly give it a very natural appearance.

Because the house is on a hill, I decided to terrace the sloping land around it in order to create flat areas for gardens around the house. At the top level, I made a shaded dining terrace on the south side, paved with terracotta tiles. There are beds full of box topiary against the house, and a large metal pergola covered with wisteria and roses. This leads to the rectangular garden outside the drawing room, with a seat at the south end which faces down the length of the terrace. The design is simple:

Above *Iris* 'Henna Stitches'
Right The courtyard formed by the original house and the new guest and staff wings has little depth of soil below it, so it is paved, and inset with beds of lavender and box, which can thrive in these conditions, clipped into topiary shapes. I like the simplicity of topiary for an entrance courtyard.

Above I designed the herb garden to be within easy reach of the kitchen, and placed orange trees in pots in the four corners, surrounded by a variety of herbs. It is a small intimate area, so I created an intricate formal layout with paths in pretty patterns of brick, stone and pebbles, and beds edged with bricks on edge. It is always nice to have a seat in a herb garden where you can sit surrounded by scent on a summer's evening.

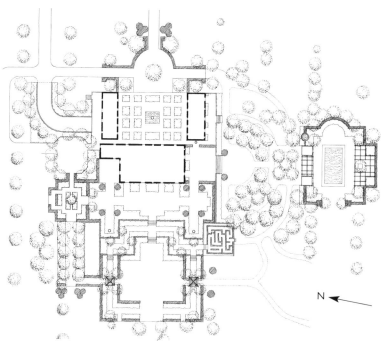

Above The garden plan.

a green lawn surrounded by predominantly white planting in stepped borders which contain *Rosa* 'Iceberg', *R.* 'Sea Pearl', *Artemisia* 'Powis Castle', *Agapanthus africanus* 'Albus', *Lavandula* 'Alba', and *L. stoechas*, various potentillas, *Lupinus arboreus* 'Albus', *Daphne* × *burkwoodii* and *Lagerstroemia* 'Nivea'. On either side of the paved areas leading from the house are *Rosmarinus officinalis* 'Miss Jessopp's Upright', with *Santolina serratifolia* and more roses. Against the walls of the house are planted *Pandorea jasminoides*, *Trachelospermum jasminoides*, climbing *Rosa brunonii* 'La Mortola', climbing *R.* 'Sombreuil', and *Cestrum nocturnum* for scent. There are cypress trees, planted in groups of three at the corners of the house and terrace to frame and give definition to the area. Cypress hedges also enclose the terrace which, on the north side, leads on to a prettily paved, geometrically patterned herb garden. Immediately outside the drawing room windows, the border is broken up by small paved areas which I designed as places for garden pots – this has turned out to be a good, practical idea as the pots are then always replaced in the same position, and the lawn is not damaged. On the western edge, in a line from the two side terraces, two viewing areas designed in the form of bastion-like projections jut outwards into the landscape; the grass extends into them and they are bordered with pleached limes.

From the centre of the white terrace, steps lead down to a narrow gravelled terrace that follows the lines of the upper terrace, hugging the sides of the bastions. The planting around this walk ranges across a blue-purple spectrum that includes *Echium candicans*, ceanothus, *Convolvulus sabatius*, caryopteris and *Melianthus major*; I have mixed these blues with silver-leaved herbaceous and other plants such as *Hibiscus syriacus* 'Oiseau Bleu', pale blue and dark blue iris such as 'Storm Centre', 'Praise the Lord' and 'Symphony', *Penstemon heterophyllus*, salvia, *Vitex agnus-castus*, and *Perovskia* 'Blue Spire'. On the walls are *Rosa* 'Veilchenblau' and *R.* 'Bleu Magenta', *Rosmarinus officinalis* Prostratus Group and *Eryngium hirsutum*. I also planted four olive trees each side for their silver-grey leaves, as well as to make a link with the olive trees in the landscape.

From here a central flight of steps leads down to a simple expanse of lawn, which is enclosed by a walk between double borders, each backed by a myrtle hedge. The walk is reached by steps from either side of the blue terrace, and the planting here is predominantly pink, with roses, pink lavender and dianthus. Halfway along each side of the walk is a shady interlude where four standard *Malus tschonoskii* surround an arbour planted with *Wisteria floribunda* 'Rosea', *Clematis* 'Perle d'Azur' and *C.* 'H. F. Young'. A gap in the walk on the west side leads the eye to the view beyond.

To the north is a garden of scented shrubs and a walk lined with *Cercis siliquastrum* f. *albida* and olive trees, underplanted with blue, brown, yellow, maroon, purple, pink and ochre irises. To the south, steps from the dining terrace lead to a semicircular lawn, lined with a crescent of umbrella pines, and on to the swimming pool.

La Bandiera was in a wonderful position, and my overriding aim in designing the garden was to keep the views of the vast landscape beyond it, leading on to the sea. So all the garden areas have open views, although, because it is hot and sunny, each terrace also has shaded places – pergolas, pleached lime walks and arbours. The planting is simple but elegant – each terrace has a colour theme – and outside the more manicured terraces and on the south side of the house I planted clumps of trees to lead into the landscape. The Marchese likes trees, so I planted *Carpinus betulus*, *Ostrya carpinifolia*, *Catalpa bignonioides*, *Malus baccata*, *M. floribunda* and *Prunus avium*. However, on the whole I have concentrated throughout the garden on using local trees such as the parasol pine *Pinus pinea*, and *Cupressus sempervirens*, as well as olives, so that though there is a distinction between the garden and the landscape, it has been achieved without too sharp a contrast.

Pages 188–9

Top left The lower terrace consists of a calm, wide expanse of lawn, in a cruciform shape, surrounded by a predominantly pink planting. Steps lead down to it from the blue-bordered terrace, and opposite, at the far end of the lawn, a wide gap in the borders allows an uninterrupted view to the landscape beyond.

Top right The iris walk planted with, among others, *Iris* 'Blue Sapphire', lemon-yellow 'McDade', ochre 'Radiant Summit' and 'Henna Stitches', brown 'New Rainbow', rosy-purple 'Pagan Royal', pink 'Sumptuous Pink' and 'Beverly Sills' and dark maroon-red 'Royal Trumpeter'. Beyond is the scented garden.

Bottom left A walk bounded by planting and hedges of myrtle leads gently down and encloses the lower terrace. On each side, halfway down, is a shady arbour planted with wisteria and clematis and sheltering a seat, where gaps in the borders allow views across the lawn.

Bottom right The predominantly blue planting on the lower terrace includes *Iris* 'Storm Centre', *Echium fastuosum* and perovskia. *Convolvulus mauritanicus* spills on to the gravel path.

Below The pretty, terracotta-tiled dining terrace is shaded by a large pergola covered with climbers including *Wisteria sinensis*, *Trachelospermum jasminoides*, *Rosa* 'Maréchal Neil' and the Banksian rose. It is furnished with pots and small box topiary in beds, and standard *Viburnum carlocephalum* provides punctuation on either side of the shutters and French windows. *Rosa* 'Cooperi'is trained on the wall.

TERRACES IN A SMALL GARDEN
Calle Somontes

This small garden is perched high on a hill in a wooded area of Madrid. The land sloped very steeply and the overgrown garden seemed to drop away from the house without relating to it, so my principal endeavour in landscaping was to give the house some breathing space by pushing new terraces outwards and by curving the paths and steps between them so that they sloped down less abruptly. The client is a passionate gardener and, as she wanted, I filled the garden with roses, lavender and irises. I used the soaring forms of cypresses throughout as punctuation points to frame views and give structure to the planting.

I created small gardens round the house. Two semicircular terraces on the same level as the house relate to the living areas. One, which runs along the length of the house, is more densely planted, with box-edged beds filled with *Rosa* 'Felicia' and a semicircular border round the edge. The main terrace, outside the drawing room, is more open, with a wide lawn and an elegant pergola at the end which provides a shady viewpoint and sitting area. Steps curve down to the swimming-pool terrace, which is also reached by a winding gravel path from the entrance courtyard on the other side of the house. The end of the pool echoes the contour of the terrace, which is also semicircular – I used the shape because it gives a bigger feeling of space. Yellow rose 'Graham Thomas' is mixed with silvers and asphodel in the swimming-pool borders.

Above, clockwise from top left *Pyrus salicifolia* 'Pendula' and *Rosa* 'Felicia' in box-edged beds outside the bedroom of the house; the swimming pool garden with *Rosa banksiae* and *R.* 'Gloire de Dijon' over the walls; procumbent roses 'Pink Bells' and 'Seafoam' with *Ceanothus thyrsiflorus* over the wall that follows the steps down; an urn as an eye-catcher in a niche at the end of curved beds. **Right** The classical pergola at the end of the main, lawned terrace framed by cypresses with roses 'Cécile Brünner', 'Penelope' and other old-fashioned roses which do well in Madrid. *Leptospermum argenteum* rises above the roses.

A COUNTRY GARDEN IN TOWN

Serrano

The building of a new guest house, gym, paddle tennis court and swimming pool necessitated the complete redesign of this formerly old and charming garden in the middle of Madrid. The main challenge as I saw it was to try to give back a country feel to a garden that had been rudely colonized by buildings. I decided to garden every bit I could get my hands on: there are hedges everywhere and trellis in between and over buildings, as well as the swimming pool and paddle court, so that every structure seems to be part of the garden.

The garden was on two levels, which I decided to keep, so as to give the new garden different areas of interest. Water in the garden is a very Spanish feature which I was keen to introduce here, and so on the upper level I designed two square pools, connected by a long narrow rill with a statue at the far end. The water is surrounded by a simple paving pattern of brick on edge. To create an allée, I planted pleached hornbeams, underplanted with white irises and other white-flowering plants to enhance the cool, elegant atmosphere of the walk, which draws the eye to the statue at the end. This view is backed by evergreen hedges towards the end of the garden, behind which I planted some very large cypresses to accentuate the vista and make a focal point.

The containment and the strong axis make this area feel as if it is a garden on its own and it is only when you walk down some steps to a lower terrace that you see that there is another garden – a lawn in cruciform shape with herbaceous borders, at the end of which I designed two wooden pavilions to be placed at either side. Though they are large, their openwork design makes them appear as light and airy gazebos, with oval windows cut into the sides. These act as frames through which you see plants on one side and an urn on the other.

Throughout the garden I planted a lot of shade-loving plants and cypresses as well as large trees to hide a neighbouring house – always a problem in urban schemes. I used yellow and white flowers to brighten the shadier areas and, towards the swimming pool where it is sunnier, some pink cistus and roses. The main part of the garden is planted in white and silver. The two front borders near the house have a very geometrical form. To edge them I planted a double hedge of box with dwarf santolina in the middle – to make a pattern of green, silver and green – and in the centre of the border I used 'Iceberg' roses as they flourish in the sun. Here I placed two beautiful terracotta urns on stepped pediments, seemingly made of box; in fact they were stepped bases of concrete with the box grown around them.

Far left A narrow canal cuts through a paved walk, leading from a rectangular pool planted with waterlilies to a statue rising from *Zantedeschia aethiopica* in a second pool. The canal and the planting along it – hornbeams underplanted with white irises and *Teucrium fruticans* – creates a very strong focus.

Left For the lower part of the garden, I designed two trelliswork pavilions inspired by ones seen in America. Roses 'Sombreuil' and 'Climbing Souvenir de la Malmaison' climb over them, and clumps of *Iris pallida* 'Variegata' contrast with the rigid double box hedge, which I like to use to contain a more informal planting.

GRAPHIC GEOMETRY

No. 1 Poultry, London

The roof garden at No. 1 Poultry – Lord Palumbo's modern office building in the City of London – was unusual for us and quite a challenge, as we had to work within the restrictions imposed by the building's architecture.

The inner garden is a circular, paved court leading out from a restaurant; in the centre was a triangular-shaped void for the atrium that runs through the height of the building. From the walls 2 metres (7 feet) high surrounding the court, the architects, James Stirling, strung a pergola which we planted with wisteria and vines. Then, working within the existing geometry, we removed triangles of paving bordering the pergola to make informal beds which we filled with an all-year-round planting of trees, shrubs, roses and herbs. In the outer gardens on either side of the restaurant we planted pillars of beech, ceanothus and roses enclosed by a serpentine wall.

Two *Magnolia grandiflora* stand sentinel on either side of an opening in the circular wall which leads to the apex garden. The angular geometry of this area seemed to call for a graphic response, so the space is filled with lines of clipped box in solid ribbons, infilled with coloured gravel and reminiscent of vineyards or field furrows. On the smooth, flat, central expanse of grass, the contrasting rounded shapes of stone balls punctuate the angles in the outline of the planting.

Left In the apex garden, diners at Sir Terence Conran's rooftop restaurant can sit on the grass and be provided with picnic hampers.
Below The garden plan.

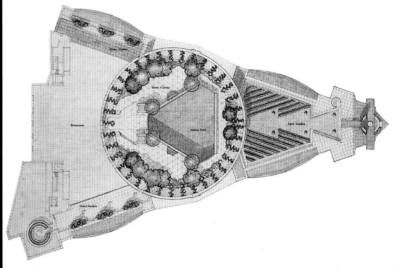

WORKING WITHIN AN HISTORIC STRUCTURE

Cheyne Walk

The layout of this historic garden – one of three belonging to the three dwellings that occupy the seventeenth-century Lindsay House in London's Chelsea – was designed by Sir Edwin Lutyens in 1911 and the shape remains essentially as he designed it: three long rectangles of grass separated by two wide stone paths with borders along the walls. The designer John Stefanidis, who was living there at the time, asked me to help him bring it back to life.

In the Lutyens design the mulberry tree, ancient even in his time, leaned over a central circular pond. The roots of the tree had now dried up the pond, and I replaced this with a solid circle of clipped box which makes an interesting change of texture, rising above the lawn. The garden is north-facing and it was, I felt, essential to have somewhere to sit in the sun, so I created two paved areas at the far end, containing wooden seats and disguised by hedges of yew separating them from the main area. The sitting areas are surrounded by beds of irises, and herbs and tall cones of small-leaved ivy in terracotta pots. This part of the garden is pleasantly secluded, and fragrant in summer, with a fig tree and a *Wisteria floribunda* 'Multijuga' trained against the far wall. Within the wall are alcoves that once contained noble statues on plinths; now topiary monkeys, created by ivy growing on wire and moss frames, add a welcome note of humour to the garden's restrained elegance.

The sitting area next to the house is a sunken courtyard, separated from the garden by a simple stone colonnade, over which grows a crimson old-fashioned rose, adding a touch of romance. I edged and furnished the courtyard and lined the steps with terracotta pots, some very large, containing clipped topiary shapes of box and bay, and with pink camellias.

The planting in the garden is simple, balanced and harmonious, and looks good all year round. Camellias are trained against the east-facing wall, and the border is underplanted with plain and variegated ivy. In the borders, box, lavender and white-variegated hostas are grown in solid rectangular blocks of contrasting colour and texture.

Clockwise from left I chose a simple combination of shapes and colour for this historic London garden: I replaced a dried-up pond with a circle of box beneath the ancient mulberry tree; ivy cones and topiary monkeys adorn the paved area; the venerable mulberry; borders, filled largely with box and *Hosta undulata* var. *albomarginata*, which is a good edging plant for a narrow border.

SMALL GARDENS
Gardens in Town

Town gardens are usually small, with the entire garden close to the house, and so I prefer to keep the overall design simple – it is better to make an impact with one strong idea, rather than diffuse attention among many less interesting ones – and to design the whole space very much in relation to the house and its view of the garden. High walls and neighbouring buildings tend to make town gardens shady, and I like to use white as a flower colour, as it looks good against a dark background and brightens the area without shocking the eye. I also find it works well to cover the walls with long-flowering, shade-loving climbers and, if the borders are narrow, to use pleached shrubs such as camellias, viburnums or fruit trees. Town gardens can frequently also be very long and narrow. If this is the case, whatever the style of the plot, the solution is to break up the length into different, distinct compartments. This device arrests the eye and gives the space an immediate interest.

Left In a town garden, functional man-made structures are often conspicuous, but here climbers soften the outline of the wrought-iron steps, while *Bupleurum fruticosum* and clipped box in a terracotta pot decorate the foot.

Right Children's play equipment need not ruin a small garden. This well-designed climbing frame in unobtrusive weathered wood is attractively set within a neat box hedge surrounded by a solid sheet of variegated ivy.

Below left In a small, shaded garden grass may not grow well and it is often better to do without a lawn. The garden need not be austere, though. In this London garden, steps lead up to a rectangle of York paving which I laid on sand and soil so that we could plant pretty rockery plants – such as *Ajuga reptans*, arabis, artemisia, thrift, veronica, violets, thymes, mint, santolina, dwarf lavender and *Sisyrinchium striatum* – between the stones.

Below A long narrow plot is best divided into different areas. Here, a rectangular lawn edged with basketweave brick gives way to a central space, with *Alchemilla mollis* at the four corners and an octagonal bed containing five *Rosa* 'Moonlight', underplanted with *Salvia pratensis* Haematodes Group and *Lavandula angustifolia* 'Hidcote'. Beyond is an informal area with a soft carpet of flower-covered grass and the atmosphere of a woodland glade. A wooden seat acts as a focal point.

Above, left In a small garden, it is a good idea to keep the planting simple and bold, for maximum impact. Here an air of elegant, harmonious balance is created by the repeated, generous clumps of white-variegated hostas, *Hosta fortunei* 'Francee', its bright tone and rounded form contrasting with the smooth, straight lines of the lawn and the solid square shapes of clipped box.

Above, right You can fit a formal design such as a parterre or knot into the smallest of spaces, and it will be attractive in every season. I filled this tiny plot, only 3.5 × 2.5 metres (11 × 8 feet), with a pattern of clipped box-edged beds, filled with herbs and summer flowers. Standard box balls on slender stems add vertical interest and definition.

Below, left In town the garden is often the only view to be seen from the house, so it is particularly important that it should look good all year round. A design using geometric lines of evergreen hedging, as in this garden (or the herb garden above right) always works well. This garden is seen from the first floor, above, so I designed an architectural pattern of clipped yew and box that is satisfying to look down on as well as to walk around.

Below, right Features more usually found in grander gardens can be scaled down and used in small ones, and one bold idea in a small space is often very effective. I love the idea of looking through a tunnel of green into a sunny space beyond, so, in a narrow dark corridor at the side of a house, I made this laburnum walk, which is as pleasing as other more famous ones, although it is only about 3.5 metres (11 feet) long.

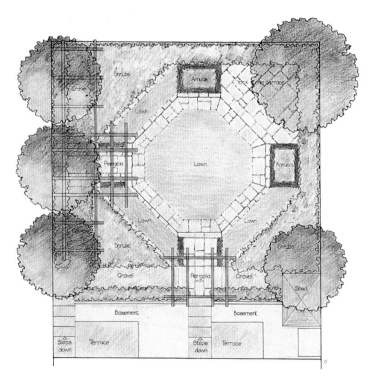

Above An octagon with corner borders overflowing with plants and shrubs gives a slightly countrified effect in a small space. In the design I did for this tiny garden – 10 square metres (35 square feet) – three triangular beds surround a lawn crossed and inset with brick paving that leads to a York stone sitting area in the fourth corner. The garden is overlooked, so I added two pergolas covered with clematis, honeysuckle and roses to provide some privacy.

Left La Limonaia, originally the lemon house for a larger house, stands on a hill above Florence with an amazing view of the Duomo and central Florence. When I was asked to design the gardens, my main concern was to create a picture that would lead the eye towards but not compete with this incredible panorama. So I designed a very simple, architectural garden. I surrounded the rectangular lawn with a border in which blocks of yew mark the entrances and the corners; each block is 1 metre (3 feet) square with a box ball in the centre – the contrasting textures creating a very satisfying effect. The rest of the border is filled with a simple planting of white agapanthus, lavender and white 'Iceberg' roses. That was all – a combination of very few design elements which looks exuberant and interesting and yet does not detract from the view.

Right, above Because this garden in Paris contains tall chestnut trees and is surrounded by high walls, making it extremely shady, I had to plant shrubs – such as mahonia and viburnum – that have good shape and attractive leaves, with annuals and tender perennials such as impatiens contributing flowers later in the season. The design is restrained, with a lawn surrounding an existing stone-edged pool, while beyond the seating area under the trees, two domed gazebos are linked by a pergola.

Right, below In this London garden, climbers, shrubs and trees clothe the boundary so densely that you can forget you are in a city. A typical long rectangular plot, it was designed as a series of three more or less circular glades, with borders closing in and then opening out again, leading you on and creating enticing hidden areas. The planting was lush and romantic, full of my favourite old-fashioned roses and ramblers.

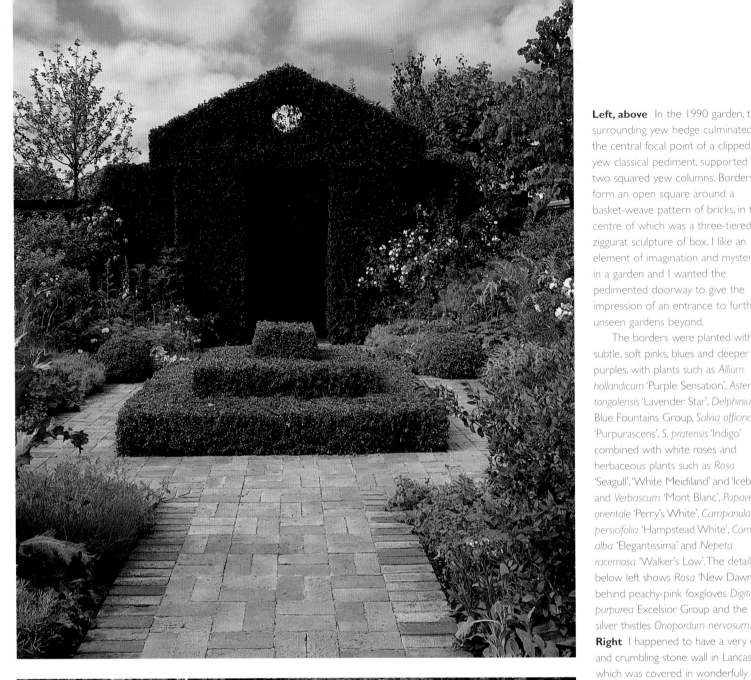

Left, above In the 1990 garden, the surrounding yew hedge culminated in the central focal point of a clipped yew classical pediment, supported by two squared yew columns. Borders form an open square around a basket-weave pattern of bricks, in the centre of which was a three-tiered ziggurat sculpture of box. I like an element of imagination and mystery in a garden and I wanted the pedimented doorway to give the impression of an entrance to further, unseen gardens beyond.

The borders were planted with subtle, soft pinks, blues and deeper purples, with plants such as *Allium hollandicum* 'Purple Sensation', *Aster tongolensis* 'Lavender Star', *Delphinium* Blue Fountains Group, *Salvia officinalis* 'Purpurascens', *S. pratensis* 'Indigo' combined with white roses and herbaceous plants such as *Rosa* 'Seagull', 'White Meidiland' and 'Iceberg' and *Verbascum* 'Mont Blanc', *Papaver orientale* 'Perry's White', *Campanula persicifolia* 'Hampstead White', *Cornus alba* 'Elegantissima' and *Nepeta racemosa* 'Walker's Low'. The detail below left shows *Rosa* 'New Dawn' behind peachy-pink foxgloves *Digitalis purpurea* Excelsior Group and the silver thistles *Onopordum nervosum*.

Right I happened to have a very old, and crumbling stone wall in Lancashire, which was covered in wonderfully coloured moss and lichen, and we also had a very good Lancastrian stone mason, so I asked him to use the stone to build the ruined tower for my 1993 garden. We built it in numbered sections, so that when we transported it to London and brought it on to the site by crane, it resembled a giant's jigsaw, which just had to be pieced together. It looked very natural surrounded by birch trees with *Rosa* 'Paul's Scarlet Climber' growing over it and arum lilies (*Zantedeschia aethiopica* 'Crowborough') nestling at its foot. This was my favourite Chelsea garden because it was so simple and natural.

CHELSEA GARDENS

Chelsea 1990 and 1993

Designing a garden for the Royal Horticultural Society's annual show at Chelsea is wonderful because I sketch a design and see it immediately realized. I have always considered my Chelsea gardens as real gardens, not stage sets, and they are opportunities for me to express myself in a way that I cannot when designing for clients. With a trusting sponsor, I have been fortunate to be able to do what I want; Chelsea is probably the most truthful image of what my designs are, because the gardens there come straight from my heart. I have been privileged to win Gold Medals for all my Chelsea gardens.

In 1990 I designed a small town garden for the *Daily Telegraph*. I was determined to have a planted garden with hedges round it, not a lot of hard landscape, so I planned a small brick-paved terrace with a pavilion, looking down on a path surrounded by wide borders. In those days you couldn't find ready-grown hedges, but John Metcalf made me a hedge of yew stuck into a frame of chicken wire, as well as providing the plants and helping me plant them.

In 1993, again for the *Daily Telegraph*, I designed a romantic semi-wild woodland inspired by one of my favourite gardens, Ninfa, in the Roman countryside, which has ruins, roses and a river running through. The space we had was long and rectangular, and I placed a ruined tower at the back as if on an island. A small stream, straddled by a turfed stone bridge, wound round the island and on, down, to the front of the garden, where it vanished beneath a rustic bridge. Near the water I planted *Iris sibirica*, with arum lilies close to the foot of the tower. On either bank I planted a grove of birches, of every age and height, and, beneath the trees, naturalized woodland plants like cranesbill, Solomon's seal, periwinkle and ferns.

CHELSEA GARDENS
Chelsea 1995

This garden, again for the *Daily Telegraph*, commemorated one hundred years of the National Trust. I wanted to have the most luscious planting you can think of, so on each side of a lawn I made a gigantic herbaceous border with enormous Irish yews, at least 5 metres (16 feet) high and 2.5 metres (8 feet) wide, planted at intervals. *Rosa* 'Iceberg' and other roses climbed up them. The borders were enclosed on one side by a copper beech hedge with *Cotinus coggygria* 'Royal Purple' planted at intervals in front. I divided the long narrow site with a black-painted pergola supporting white wisteria and, beyond, a beautiful wall built in old Cumbrian slate – the only hard feature – through which you glimpse an urn set in a birch glade behind. In a way, the design was a progression from the woodland garden I had done before: here, one walked out of the woodland through an opening in the wall into a more formal herbaceous garden. In the centre of the lawn were three fountains – polished squares of Cumbrian slate, each slightly larger than the other, linked by a slate-lined rill. In the centre of each square, water bubbled up and over the slate. I found the juxtaposition of the old traditional slate wall and the modern design in polished slate very satisfying.

Opposite I wanted a bold planting scheme for the herbaceous borders, so I chose to have all the plants in red and white with different shades of green and burgundy. At the far end: *Hesperis matronalis* var. *albiflora* is behind *Hebe subalpina* and *Cytisus* 'Boskoop Beauty'. *Centaurea cyanus* 'Black Boy' is coming into flower next to *Lupin* 'Noble Maiden'. 'The Times Rose' is behind *Incarvillea delavayi* 'Snowdrop'. *Hosta fortunei* 'Francee' is at each corner of the beds.

Left, above *Hesperis matronalis* var. *albiflora* is behind *Cynara cardunculus*. *Lupinus* 'Noble Maiden' and *Rosa* 'Iceberg' draw the eye towards *Cornus alba* 'Elegantissima' and 'The Times Rose' below.

Left, below *Iris* 'White Swirl' beside red *Dahlia* 'Bednall Beauty', with feathery *Foeniculum vulgare* and the beautiful leaves of *Beta vulgaris* 'Bull's Blood'.

CHELSEA GARDENS

Chelsea 1998

The next garden that I designed at Chelsea for the *Evening Standard* in 1998 was based on one I had done in Normandy France some years before. I particularly wanted to have a lot of water – because water is so pretty in the confined spaces that are the Chelsea plots – and to use Portland stone, which I had never done in England. I had also recently been to Japan, where I was very much inspired by the sophistication and simplicity of their garden design, combined with the austerity of their materials – they use so few, and every item is made to count.

The rectangular plots at Chelsea – so similar in shape to the typical town garden – are often made more appealing if divided into different areas, and I thought it would add further interest if the garden were on different levels. At the back of the garden, a mixed planting of woodland shrubs, together with the existing tall plane trees on the Chelsea site, gave the impression of a forest canopy. Beneath were two squares of pleached lime on either side of a stainless-steel water sculpture by William Pye, which was set in a narrow canal edged in Portland stone. The pleached limes made a frame for the sculpture, which seemed to emerge from the woods and water like a lone sentinel.

The canal carried the water out of the trees, continuing through two tightly planted broad herbaceous borders, and flowed into the first of two pools, again edged with the pale

broad blocks of Portland stone. This pool was square, set in the centre of an area plainly furnished with grass either side, and bordered on one side with a yew hedge. From there the water ran in a broad cascade down stone steps, inset into wider grass steps edged with clipped box, and narrowing slightly in width, fell eventually into the lowest pool. This area contained nothing but the shimmering rectangular pool set directly into a calm green lawn. The entire site seemed to be filled with water, the pools and grass giving an air of calm, and the woods and sculpture adding a sense of mystery or hidden meaning. The whole garden was a combination of various elements, which I had used several times in other gardens, but here they were simplified and pared down to convey a contemporary simplicity. I think this garden was particularly successful, and I was delighted when it was awarded 'Best in Show' for 1998.

Opposite A canal carries the water through substantial herbaceous borders planted with *Heuchera* 'Rachel' at the corner of the bed. *Verbascum* 'Helen Johnson' and *V. chaixii* 'Cotswold Queen' rise in front of *Achillea* 'Moonshine' and *Hesperis matronalis* var. *albiflora*. *Verbascum* × *phoenicum* 'Gainsborough' is planted at the back with *Miscanthus sinensis* 'Silberfeder'. *Stipa gigantea* weaves through the length of the border, with geums and *Iris* 'Deep Black' in front.
Below The water cascades down stone steps into the lowest rectangular pool set in a calm green lawn. The perfect size of the herbaceous borders is all-important in this garden of balance and precision. If you walked round the side of the plot, you could see that the space at the back was a simple, separate cloistered room, where the pleached lime squares surrounded square grass mounds on each side of the canal.

CHELSEA GARDENS
Chelsea 2000

Over the years I think that my designs for Chelsea have become simpler, and more contemporary. In each of my gardens I have tried to do things which may be traditional in concept but are definitely modern in execution, and I particularly enjoy experimenting with colour there.

The most recent garden that I did at Chelsea in 2000 for the *Evening Standard* was a development of the previous garden, but turned inside out; instead of having water set in the middle of grass I decided to have grass in the middle of water – an island of grass surrounded by a rectangular, deep moat. The idea was to walk through two deep, square herbaceous borders, over a large stepping stone into the central area. This was very simple and peaceful – only grass, with olive trees in huge containers set into the moat so that they looked as though they were floating in the water. Crossing the water at the end you stepped through a square metal arch to a more planted area with a sculpture, once again by William Pye, placed on a grass mound, and surrounded by long grasses and herbaceous plants, with groupings of three tall cypresses placed near the four corners for structure.

Above Irises 'Indian Chief' and 'Caliente' with *Allium hollandicum* 'Purple Sensation'.
Right *Papaver orientale* 'Orangeade Maison', iris, *Geum* 'Mrs J. Bradshaw' and *Anchusa azurea* 'Loddon Royalist' mingle in this array of colours. *Verbascum chaixii* 'Album' and *V.* 'Cotswold Beauty' are planted with no regularity in this border and *Allium hollandicum* 'Purple Sensation' looks as if it has self-seeded all over. *Artemesia* 'Powis Castle' and *Trifolium repens* 'Purpurascens' edge the border.